"Reading this book is like havii
that faculty rarely have. . . . I an
[It is] perfect for busy teachers and students. . . . It should be required reading for every person in charge of faculty development and a required book for all young Christian professors." [from the foreword]

—**Dr. Perry L. Glanzer**, professor of educational foundations; editor-in-chief, *Christian Scholar's Review*; resident scholar, Baylor Institute for Studies of Religion, Baylor University

"This is a terrific book—wonderful wisdom, integrated theory and praxis, honesty with transparency, captivating stories, and reflective teaching insights. A must-read for new and veteran professors."

—**Dr. Tim Detwiler**, provost, Kuyper College

"Dr. Schultze's book will inspire *all* teachers, from adult Sunday school to K–12 and universities, to love God more, to love students more, and to risk being a more authentic and vulnerable servant teacher."

—**Shirley V. Hoogstra**, president, Council for Christian Colleges & Universities

"This book is practical, pithy, faith-infused, and rooted in long classroom experience and genuine empathy for students. It offers a conversation about your classroom from which you will emerge with fresh food for thought and a wealth of practical suggestions."

—**David I. Smith**, director, Kuyers Institute for Christian Teaching and Learning, Calvin University

"Wow! This personal, practical, and engaging book from a master teacher is the encouragement every professor needs for these challenging times."

—**Dr. Elizabeth McLaughlin**, professor, Bethel University (IN)

"I. LOVE. THIS. BOOK! Dr. Schultze's practical insights, gained from decades of success (and failure) in his efforts to serve students, help all of us in Christian higher education to follow our calling more intentionally."

—**Dr. Karl Payton**, associate vice president—accreditation & quality assurance, LeTourneau University

"This is a marvelous book—personal, accessible, pithy, and loaded with practical ideas for faculty in all disciplines. I just read it while planning a new course; it made a tremendous difference."

—**Dr. Kevin Schut**, professor and chair, Trinity Western University

"Dr. Schultze offers instructors at every career stage much hard-won wisdom in candid and sapient reflections illuminated by vivid and humble vignettes. It's the best book on teaching I've read in a long while, and I plan to reread it and recommend it widely."

—**Dr. John G. Stackhouse Jr.**, Samuel J. Mikolaski Professor of Religious Studies and dean of faculty development, Crandall University, Moncton, New Brunswick, Canada

"This book brings a hopeful, holistic approach to teaching with a commitment to virtue and spiritual health. Schultze helps professors renew their callings with much practical wisdom and the heart of a servant mentor."

—**Dr. Annalee Ward**, professor, director of the Wendt Center for Character Education, University of Dubuque

"This book is a rare find, a book that should be required reading for Christian educational pedagogy courses, both within a major at a Christian institution and also within the education departments that offer credentialing and certifications for teaching excellence as required by all institutions of learning."

—**Dr. Todd V. Lewis**, professor emeritus, Biola University

"This book is amazing—inspiring, relatable, practical without being preachy. It provides plenty of guidance for how I can move forward as a better teacher—a servant teacher. I plan to discuss it with my colleagues."

—**Dr. Seth Hamman**, professor, director of the Center for Advancement of Cybersecurity, Cedarville University

"I encourage all experienced and new teachers to read prayerfully through this book with others. Servant teaching can transform your students and make a lasting impact."

—**Dr. John Pauly**, former provost, Eastern University

"This book should be required to be read, studied, and discussed at all new-faculty orientations and retreats. It is a persuasive and encouraging call to remember that why and how we teach matters."

—**Dr. Tom Carmody**, professor, Vanguard University

"I loved reading this book! Each of the thirty short chapters is replete with practical wisdom to be applied in the classroom, applied in course preparations, and in the process of student appraisals. The book takes seriously the biblical mandate of faithfully cultivating the garden that is our classroom."

—**Dr. Paul Patton**, professor emeritus, Spring Arbor University

"I couldn't put the book down. With his genuine warmth and sincerity, Schultze offers remarkably practical and faith-inspiring practices for creating classrooms that foster a love of learning. I appreciate Schultze's transparency in sharing his successes and struggles as a teacher, and what we can all learn from his experiences. *Servant Teaching* shows that Schultze is one of the most important voices in Christian higher education. Every educator must read this amazing book."

—**Dr. Diane Badzinski**, professor, Colorado Christian University

"This is exactly the book I have long wanted—short yet power-packed vignettes that can be used by teachers who've been at it a long time to freshen or sharpen their teaching as well as by those new to the craft who need to get their bearings and a plan to grow into a great teacher. I can't wait to get it in the hands of our faculty!"

—**Dr. Ryan Hartwig**, vice president for academic affairs and provost, Vanguard University

"This wonderfully readable book helps clarify what faith integration is and provides very useful tips on how to engage and grow students of faith while navigating course content. Dr. Schultze's vulnerability and transparency are convicting and enlightening."

—**Dr. Kevin Jones**, professor, George Fox University

"Schultze delivers amazing insights for Christian educators who care about transforming student (and faculty) lives. No matter where you are in your teaching journey, you will be encouraged and your pockets will be filled with proven servant teaching practices."

—**Dr. Robert H. Woods Jr.**, executive director, Christianity and Communication Studies Network (www.theccsn.com)

"Many books on Christian pedagogy have appeared in recent years, but what we really need are actual examples. *Servant Teaching* provides such practical insights and a wealth of real-life examples of what it means to teach with faith, skill, and virtue. It will inspire and instruct Christian professors."

—**Dr. Rick Ostrander**, assistant to the president for global education, innovation and new program development, Westmont College

"On every Robert Graham piece of clothing there are embroidered three words: Knowledge, Wisdom, Truth. On every page of Quentin Schultze's *Servant Teaching* there are embedded priceless pedagogical gems of knowledge, wisdom, and truth, as well as hard-won tips on how to turn information into knowledge, and knowledge into wisdom, and wisdom into truth. If you're involved in Christian higher education in any way, this book will change your life."

—**Dr. Leonard Sweet**, author, professor, publisher, and founder of preachthestory.com

"Wisely, Quentin starts his book with the practice of gratitude. I'm grateful not only for his lifelong dedication to Christian education, but his willingness to share his insight, passion, and mastery with us! What a gift."

—**Dr. Tim Muehlhoff**, professor, Biola University, co-director, Winsome Conviction Project

"This is the book I should have read when I started teaching over 35 years ago. Of the literature on theology and pedagogy, there is nothing like it. It is simple yet profound, with deep and practical theological insights into teaching. Schultze provides a method and model of Christian virtue. Buy it and read it; this book will not disappoint."

—**Dr. Benson P. Fraser**, Westminster Canterbury Fellow for Religious Studies and Lifelong Learning, Virginia Wesleyan University

"I continue to be inspired by the competence and real-world winsomeness that Quentin Schultze brings to his writing, teaching, and the relational dimensions of life. I found *Servant Teaching* to be an encouragement to my soul, and trust that other readers will experience the same. The short chapters in this book are accessible and inspiring, and offer a treasure-trove of insights gained through observation and experience by one of the master teachers among us. We are fortunate that Quentin felt called, even compelled, as he looked back over his long and distinguished career, to synthesize life lessons about 'how to inspire and encourage our students to become faithful, lifelong learners.'"

—**Dr. Karen Longman**, professor, program director for the PhD in higher education, Azusa Pacific University

"In a world of dramatic change in higher education, this book provides the renewal and inspiration we need. Students will benefit from the growth and passion *Servant Teaching* provides. Faculty will appreciate its practical and honest approach. Thank you, Dr. Schultze, for this outstanding and inspirational resource. It is a masterpiece."

—**Dr. Stephanie Bennett**, professor, director of wordship, Palm Beach Atlantic University

Selected Books by Quentin J. Schultze

Communicating with Grace and Virtue:
Learning to Listen, Speak, Text, and Interact as a Christian

An Essential Guide to Interpersonal Communication:
Building Great Relationships with Faith, Skill, and Virtue
(with Diane M. Badzinski)

Résumé 101: A Student and Recent Grad Guide to Crafting
Résumés and Cover Letters That Land Jobs

Here I Am: Now What on Earth Should I Be Doing?

High-Tech Worship? Using Presentational Technologies
Wisely

An Essential Guide to Public Speaking:
Serving Your Audience with Faith, Skill, and Virtue

Christianity and the Mass Media in America:
Toward a Democratic Accommodation

Habits of the High-Tech Heart:
Living Virtuously in the Information Age

Communicating for Life:
Christian Stewardship in Community and Media

Televangelism and American Culture:
The Business of Popular Religion

American Evangelicals and the Mass Media

Servant Teaching

Practices for Renewing Christian Higher Education

Quentin J. Schultze

Foreword by
Perry L. Glanzer

Edenridge Press LLC
Grand Rapids, Michigan

Published by
Edenridge Press LLC
Grand Rapids, Michigan USA
service@edenridgepress.com
Quantity discount pricing is available.

Edited by Robert Banning, Turning Leaves Editorial.
Cover design by Matthew Plescher.

Schultze, Quentin J.
   Title: Servant teaching: practices for renewing
   Christian higher education / Quentin J. Schultze;
   foreword by Perry L. Glanzer

Library of Congress Control Number: 2022943675

ISBN 978-1-937532-00-0 (alk. Paper)

   EDU029100
   EDUCATION / Teaching / Methods & Strategies

   Subjects: LCSH: Teaching—Religious aspects—
   Christianity. | Teachers—Religious life. | Education
   (Christian theology) | Christian education—Teaching
   methods.

Dedication

To Robert H. Woods Jr., who diligently carries the mantle of communication studies in Christian higher education.

And to David I. Smith, who creatively pursues faith-shaped pedagogy for Christian educators.

Acknowledgments

My debts are broad and deep, but as my dedication suggests, I owe special thanks to Robert H. Woods Jr. and David I. Smith, outstanding teacher-scholars in Christian higher education who served me well by tirelessly modeling servanthood.

Many friends and colleagues reviewed book drafts, including Jonathan Pettigrew, Seth Hamman, Tim Detwiler, Stephanie Bennett, Thomas Mach, Elizabeth McLaughlin, Mark Fackler, Karen Longman, Robert Gustafson, David I. Smith, Ryan Hartwig, and Karl Payton. Special thanks to Perry Glanzer, an exceptional education scholar, for writing the foreword.

Bob Banning of Turning Leaves Editorial served me splendidly as a trusted advisor as well as editor.

Sid Jansma Jr.'s generous support was essential for this project.

For over three decades I taught at Calvin University in Grand Rapids, Michigan. The students there helped me learn how to teach with faith, skill, and virtue.

Some of the people I quote in this book are writers whose works have significantly shaped me as a Christian teacher-scholar. These include Dietrich Bonhoeffer, Eugene H. Peterson, Henri J. M. Nouwen, Abraham J. Heschel, Nicholas Wolterstorff, Søren Kierkegaard, James M. Houston, Elie Wiesel, C. S. Lewis, Augustine of Hippo, Wendell Berry, Robert K. Greenleaf, and Paul Tournier.

Contents

Notes

Foreword

From the start, and then throughout, this book does something that few books about Christian education do.

It captures the reality that teaching evokes strong emotions, a reality that surprised me when I started teaching. I can remember coming back from one of my first adjunct teaching courses—an adult weekend class taught from 6 to 10 on Friday night and 8 to 4 on Saturday for two straight weekends—and just lying on the floor stewing over, feeling shame about, and regretting various pedagogical choices. Feeling like a fraud, unable to keep students engaged for hours on end, I wondered if I should just go ahead and give up on teaching. What was true for me in those moments was what author Quentin Schultze notes of himself in his early career: "I was seeking earthly perfection, rather than realistic excellence."

Quentin says he authored this book to encourage us, and—in my own reading—he accomplished that goal. I sensed he had experienced the same despair and frustration we all experience as educators when we take our students and subject seriously. Yet, like a master teacher, Quentin moves us beyond our paralyzing emotional responses to deeper spiritual, character, and skill formation—what he calls "servant teaching."

What is noteworthy about Quentin's approach is that he knows the motivations from which excellent Christian teaching should spring. In stark contrast to most pedagogical books, rather than starting with shallow tips and techniques, he allows his practical insights to flow *from* this rightly ordered motivation. He also knows how to speak theologically about teaching—as a skill that always needs sharpening among Christian teachers.

He then intentionally shifts readers away from a focus on our own emotional issues and toward a focus on students and their emotions and needs—looking beyond one's insecurities, suggesting even sharing one's own insecurities and wounds with students. He knows that students long for this kind of care and authenticity. At a recent dinner, I was reminded of Quentin's valuable insights as my oldest son told me all about the professors he liked and did not like. Not surprisingly, the professors he liked demonstrated unique care for him as a person and his context. Quentin guides us in how to foster these fundamental compassionate and emotional connections with our students.

He then goes on to do what a good mentor does. He provides the practical wisdom that he uses throughout class. These are not the generalized moral principles, or even the general virtues, often presented in pedagogy textbooks. Instead, Quentin offers wisdom—the deep reflections upon teaching practice of someone excellent in his field. He clearly has thought long and hard about the full range of his teaching practices, and we gain from his wise mentorship as he guides us through his thinking, longings, and actions. Reading this book is like having that wise, older teaching mentor that faculty rarely have (I certainly did not).

I will give a couple examples where his wisdom resonated with my own experience. In the chapter entitled "Foster Applied Learning," Quentin opens with the simple but profound point, "When students see how my courses will help them to serve others, they are more grateful and motivated." I had a similar experience when I started asking my graduate students to participate in interviews for our Baylor University Faith and Character Study. Not only do they learn from students directly, instead of simply reading books about students being interviewed; they appreciate the fact that the results contribute to changes in how Baylor approaches moral and spiritual development. Indeed, these interviews even contributed to the restructuring of chapel. As Quentin insightfully observes, students do not like busywork. They appreciate work that makes them better servants.

Second, Quentin advises readers to teach from their strengths. I remember being frustrated with a teacher with whom I was coteaching who did not show up for the first class until its exact start. He then made an amazingly effective dramatic entrance. I realized that he was using his drama background in his pedagogy. I then tried the same sort of dramatic entrance the next semester, and it completely flopped. As Quentin notes, "Students are best served when we all pursue our strengths." Readers of this book will not have to learn some of these lessons the hard way.

Of course, veteran teachers also have much to gain in reading this text. For instance, I found Quentin's particular practice of how to acquire quick, early student feedback an improvement over my own approaches and plan to try it soon. The need to continually improve our teaching is as urgent as ever, and Quentin's book is a helpful resource in pursuit of the growth and development of young and veteran teachers alike.

I am profoundly grateful for this book that will be ideal for the Teaching and Learning class we offer to our graduate students. Quentin adds to the great pedagogical tradition of

Calvin University (as exemplified by David I. Smith) by giving us additional Christian wisdom. Moreover, this book is perfect for busy teachers and students. It could be read almost like a teaching devotional. Yet it eschews the tidiness of some devotional writing by avoiding simple answers and simplistic approaches. It is easy to read in short bursts, but it rewards with rich insight. It should be required reading for every person in charge of faculty development and a required book for all young Christian professors.

Perry L. Glanzer, PhD
Baylor University

Introduction

A former student wrote to tell me that she was reviewing her notes from a class I had taught decades ago. I felt blessed by her kind note.

Before she was my student, however, a disheartening experience nearly drove me out of teaching. I was administering a final exam. As students finished, they gave me their exams and departed—sometimes with a whisper of thanks for the course. One student handed me a completed exam and headed for the door without a word or even eye contact. On his way out of the room, he threw his course notes and the textbook (written by me) into the metal trash can with a resounding clang. The remaining students looked up and chuckled. I fumed. That sleepless night I wondered if I had chosen the wrong profession.

Instead of leaving teaching, however, I determined to renew my calling. This book reveals what I learned that has served my students well. The brief chapters are filled with illustrative experiences as well as biblical and theological insights. My aim is not to tell you exactly how to teach but to suggest pedagogical practices that you can adapt to your teaching style, situation, and discipline. I also reveal, as a communication scholar, how I say some things to students; I seek to capture the rhetorical flavor.

This book addresses how we can renew Christian higher education in the face of considerable obstacles. Christian philosopher Nicholas Wolterstorff says that the main challenge to Christian education "lies in the fact that many of the students whom the Christian school graduates are not at all convinced of the worth of the institution they graduated from."[1] One key to overcoming this challenge is to develop teaching that demonstrates the deep value of Christian higher education. My own teaching experiences suggest ways of moving forward faithfully in the face of today's declining enrollments and financial exigencies.

Each of us has discipline-based knowledge and skill. But how can we inspire students, including nonmajors, to acquire the knowledge and employ the skills?

I believe that we can renew Christian higher education by focusing on the three interwoven themes of this book— faith, skill, and virtue. We teach *through faith*. We teach *by skill*. We teach *with virtue*. In other words, we faithfully practice skilled teaching as virtuous persons. I call this *servant teaching—serving our students by teaching them with faith, skill, and virtue*. In the process, we serve God as well.[2]

As I describe in this book, I've practiced servant teaching in undergraduate, graduate, online, adjunct, and full-time instruction. Such servant teaching is all about intentionally integrating faith, skill, and virtue. In my experience, the benefits are many, including better-motivated students, greater learning for life, and graduates who advocate for Christian education.

We servant teachers learn from our failures as well as our successes. I've made many foolish mistakes. I've also struggled with personal issues that negatively affected my teaching. I tend to be impatient, perfectionistic, and defensive. I need to work on myself in order to serve my students well. I discovered the importance of virtue—good qualities of character. I realized that my own spiritual health is a major part of my teaching. By the grace of God, the fruit of the spirit can form our characters as servant teachers (Gal. 5:22–23).

I am convinced that the best teaching and learning occur at the intersection of our students' formation and our own formation. As faculty and students, we can shape each other to be faithful teacher-learners under God's mercy. We teachers are not just helping students build their careers—no more than we are teaching simply to advance our own academic careers. We value the personal formation of the student in the light of the discipline being taught.[3] Moreover, we teachers are also students, learning from our students how best to teach them for the benefit of God's kingdom. We and our students grow together into the kind of community that nurtures current students and attracts prospective students.

This book is about how to inspire and encourage our students to become faithful, lifelong learners. It's about how our faith can shape our pedagogy. It's about what we like and dislike about our work, including matters of the heart that we rarely discuss. And it's about why I now approach teaching with deep gratitude—even for the student who challenged me by loudly trashing his course notes and my precious textbook. He woke me up to pursue a more excellent way, which I share with you (1 Cor. 12:31).

We must continually renew our teaching. Student culture changes; we adapt. Such ongoing pedagogical renewal is essential both for how we teach and how we promote Christian higher education to prospective students and their families. As faculty, we implicitly define the meaning of our universities as distinctively Christian endeavors. When our own Christian language and educational practices grow stale, Christian education seems irrelevant to the Christian community—an unnecessary expense.

I hung on my campus office wall a John Swanson print, *The Conductor*, which metaphorically depicts God as an orchestra conductor on a stage with musicians poised for direction. I posted below the art print many photos of my graduates. Periodically I added new pictures that included wedding and employment photos, and eventually consecutive generations of former students who trusted me with their children. When prospective students and their parents visited my office, I pointed to the photo collage and talked about former students as examples of God's good works (Eph. 2:10). I wanted parents, especially, to know that I, as God's ambassador, would nurture their children. After all, I, like you, am not just a professor, but even more importantly a follower of Jesus Christ. "Christ has not appointed assistant-professors—but followers," wrote Søren Kierkegaard (1813–55).[4] I aim to assure parents and prospective students that I will faithfully nourish students' hearts and minds.

This book addresses what David I. Smith and James K. A. Smith call a lack of "nuanced accounts of how teaching and learning are supposed to work in a Christian setting."[5] Obviously my experiences are not scientifically controlled experiments. Personal teaching styles and academic disciplines will shape our teaching. There will be variations in how particular Christian schools approach teaching, partly because of different historic Christian traditions, diverse constituencies, and varied institutional parameters—from class sizes to available classroom technologies, and from types of academic programs to assorted student populations. My examples are suggestive and illustrative.

In all cases, however, faith, skill, and virtue are three essentials in Christian teaching. C. S. Lewis said, "The task of the modern educator is not to cut down jungles but to irrigate deserts."[6] I view faith, skill, and virtue as interrelated ways of irrigating our pedagogical deserts. We can teach every university subject this way. We can teach chemistry and English as well as business and computer science.

We can do it in the classroom and online, in our offices and at cafés.

Servant teaching sees instructors and students as whole persons. Therefore, I consider more than just instructional skills and techniques. I address, as Perry L. Glanzer and Nathan F. Alleman put it, "how teachers perceive their students' identities" and "understand their own motivations."[7] I aim to teach from my heart as well as mind, to teach relationally, and to be sensitive to what the Holy Spirit is doing through me and my students as we learn together.

When we are servant teachers, more students come to love learning. They see themselves as God's stewards of learning, called to learn in order to delight in serving others. We break the cycle of students who have assumed year after year that education is merely about processing information and doing busywork on the way to eventual liberation from schooling.

Students and parents resonate with servant teaching. They yearn to see a teacher's authentic faith in action. They appreciate skilled teaching that is continually improved by student feedback. They value teachers who model Christian virtue—who authentically point the way to being Christ-like servant learners. Parents desire learning that forms hearts and minds.

In my experience, students desire meaningful lives in which they can grow intellectually and affectively, navigate cultural differences, and become faithful leaders. But they are not sure how to pursue such worthy goals. We are called to model and practice it by integrating faith, skill, and virtue in our teaching.

Isn't this what we desire in our teaching—life-giving practices rather than meaning-starved routines? Henri Nouwen, who gave up an academic career for ministry, wrote, "Grades, exams, selective systems, promotion chances and desires for awards often block the manifestation of the best man can produce."[8] If true, how tragic!

Academic culture frequently fails to inspire us to enjoy our calling and celebrate the Holy Spirit's fruit along the way. Our hearts ache. We are busy but not flourishing. We suffer from the same kinds of stress as our students. Jesus says, "Come and follow me" so that we might experience an abundant life (John 1:43; John 10:10). Do we feel such deep fulfillment? Or do we miss out on this blessing by separating our spiritual growth from our teaching practices?

When we teach, what are we doing? Whom are we following? Do we sense that the Holy Spirit is accompanying us? Do we wonder why we can't seem to motivate students to love learning? How can we help students to experience learning as part of God's wondrous work in their lives, as preparation for serving others? For me, pursuing answers to these questions has been a joyous pilgrimage to servant teaching.

I wish to encourage you. We all grow discouraged when we face budget cuts, when we can't motivate students, when our lectures or discussions flop, when we read unkind comments in course evaluations (which might have just enough truth in them to sting our consciences), and especially when we wonder if we have faithfully chosen a fitting profession.

I keep a folder of notes from former students to reread when I need extra encouragement. I learn much from the letters because they often highlight what I have been doing right. They too are course evaluations. As I suggest throughout the book, listening to students is a pedagogical gift— even when students speak by tossing their semester's work into the wastebasket.

Thanks so much for joining me on the journey toward becoming a servant teacher. I know how busy you are, so I wrote thirty short chapters with illustrative practices that you can individually or collectively read, discuss, rework, and implement as appropriate.

Meanwhile, I am conducting workshops and webinars on servant teaching that go into greater depth on practices outlined in this book. Contact me with questions about this book or to be added to my mailing list, which announces upcoming workshops and webinars (just visit my website at www.quentinschultze.com).

I hope you can read and discuss this book with colleagues—openly, from your heart, with gratitude for the opportunities God has given you to nurture learning and learners. I agree with Robert K. Greenleaf, founder of the modern Servant Leadership movement, that "the prime formative challenge of our times . . . is the nurture of servants."[9] This includes you and me as well as our students. The better we serve, the more likely that our former students will reread their old course notes and recommend our schools to others.

1

Fill Your Heart with Gratitude

I begin each class session by telling students that I am glad to see them. I end every session by thanking them for coming. A student asked me why. I replied, "Because every time you come to class I am honored and blessed." "Wow," he said, "I never thought of it that way." Neither had I until I gained a deeper understanding of my calling as a servant teacher.

The most important virtue for servant teaching is gratitude. When our hearts are bathed in gratitude, we see our students and our work as wonderful gifts. We build immunity to the cynical, critical attitudes that can infect academe.

I think gratitude is the missing first chapter in books on Christian pedagogy. Before we practice our instructional skills, we need to prepare our hearts. We tend to take our work for granted. Instead of seeing it as a gift from God, we might view it as a burden imposed upon us. Our work becomes more of a duty than a gift, and more of a routine than an adventure.

Let's give thanks to God for opening the door for us to serve. Let's also thank our Lord for our students, the institution that employs us, our time and energy, our abilities, the staffs that serve us, the teachers and authors and mentors who helped us earn our academic degrees, the colleagues who support and encourage us, and even the freedom to make mistakes.

Let's add the bigger picture—the grace that saves and sustains us. We inherit the very love of God. We are God's children, called to instruct those who are grafted into the same covenantal love. The more deeply we know that we are unconditionally loved, the more deeply we can love our students.[10] "We love," John says, "because He first loved us" (1 John 4:19).

When we lose the joy of salvation, we can become joyless teachers. And our students sense this; the ways we present ourselves to them verbally and nonverbally can suggest that we are simply going through the motions of teaching, just like they might be going through the motions of learning. We need practices to help us continually renew our hearts in the light of every good gift from God.

I thank God for another day of life as soon as I wake up. I ask God to make me a blessing to others that day. Otherwise, my thoughts turn to the chores and stresses of the coming hours; my prayers become petitions without doxologies.

I associate the campus entrance sign with God's goodness. As I enter each day, I remind myself that all the buildings, instruction, and learning are gifts from God. I am there as God's guest, called and equipped. When I see the campus sign, it lifts my heart in preparation for service.

I created a gratitude board in my home office. On a corkboard I post encouraging notes from others, Scripture, photographs, thoughts, hymns, ticket stubs, and other mementos that remind me of God's abundant blessings. One photo shows me at the grave of my alcoholic father, forgiving him for abuse; overcoming my resentment toward him is an amazing gift from God. I take naps on the sofa below the gratitude board, savoring items on the board as I drift off to sleep.

I placed my gratitude board on the wall where I see it each time I leave my home office. No matter what I am doing in the office on a given day, I want to be reminded when I depart that God is in charge and has blessed my life. Finally, the gratitude board serves as a kind of benediction, reminding me when I leave the room to go forth to love and serve the Lord.

You and I are beloved recipients of many gifts. The more we recognize this, the more inclined we will be to offer our lives gratefully in the service of our students. Bernard of Clairvaux (1090–1153) wrote, "The more surely you know yourself loved, the easier you will find it to love in return."[11] Gratitude is our way of saying "yes" to God, to ward off what Søren Kierkegaard calls the "sickness" of ingratitude.[12]

Gratitude nurtures servant teaching. There is no secret formula. Our thankfulness just needs to be wholehearted. The apostle Paul says, "Rejoice in the Lord always. I will say it again: Rejoice!" (Phil. 4:4). If our attitude toward our Redeemer lacks thankfulness, then our attitude toward our students will as well. The psalmist asks, "How shall I return to the Lord for all his goodness to me?" (Ps. 116:12) We respond by praising God for every good gift, including the opportunity to be servant teachers.

Reflection
What practices help you to be a grateful servant teacher—
and what items would you put on your gratitude board?

2

Embrace Your Calling

I tell my students that for me teaching is a God-given calling. I want to remind myself as well as them why I teach. I reveal that I am still learning what it means to be called to honor God by serving students.

Calling is not just a matter of career, profession, or job. Calling is an orientation to grateful, sacrificial living. God calls us to climb out of our egos and into service. This fundamental human orientation goes back to Genesis. God creates the earth and then instructs Adam "to work it and keep it"—literally, "*serve* it and keep it" (Gen. 2:15); and the word for "work/serve" sometimes means "worship." Adam becomes God's first student and servant—and worshiper.

God gives you and me all kinds of people and resources and inspires us to care for his world. We care for our families and our churches as well as our schools. In turn, we can view all academic majors as doorways for students to enter post-graduation as servants. This "servant caring" is a way of honoring God by using all of our gifts and resources for God's glory.

We can talk about our academic work as a career, but in the bigger picture of God's plans for us we are stewards of his world, planted in schools. Just as Adam and Eve cultivated the garden of Eden, we are servants in the field of education, nurturing and growing our students in academic disciplines. Pedagogical strategies and course lessons are tools for our educational stewardship.

In other words, we are nurturers, using words, textbooks, technologies, and more to form students into God's servants. In short, we servant teachers are called to grow servant-oriented students. This is *our* meaningful work, which helps students find *their* meaningful work in God's garden. In Hebrew, the word "garden" means the "whole fecundity of the given world, this productive, potential world."[13] This is what you and I and our students inherit as God's servants.

Our calling is not just to pass along information to learners. The best servant teaching nurtures students to cultivate God's world in the service of others to God's glory.

I discovered a simple way of framing this biblical view of calling for students and myself: We followers of Jesus Christ are called to learn in order to better love God and love our neighbors as ourselves (Mark 12:30–31). This kind of love (*caritas*) has two dimensions. First, such love involves *heartfelt compassion*, "caring about" those whom we serve. In other words, we put our hearts into our actions. Second, it involves *skilled excellence*, "caring for" those whom we serve. Our calling directs us to become both compassionate and skilled servants.[14] We thereby honor God.

For example, I need to be a compassionate and excellent teacher, modeling heart and skill for students. I also need to help them become compassionate and excellent in the subjects I teach. If my students are going to become filmmakers, I direct them to be compassionate toward their production crew and their likely audiences (to serve their audiences from their hearts, desiring what's best for audiences) while also becoming highly skilled in their craft. Therefore, as a servant teacher I look for God-honoring ways of nurturing my students in both heartfelt compassion and skilled excellence. Our work becomes a form of worship.

This two-sided approach to calling helps my students grasp the idea of being a Christian in their careers. For instance, students bring up the question of what it means to be a Christian communicator, Christian social media producer, or Christian public speaker. The same questions come up when we talk more generally about what it means to be a Christian entrepreneur, Christian physician, or Christian musician. In all the occupational "gardens" of God's world, we followers of Jesus Christ are called to serve people with compassion and excellence.

I suggest to my students that Christians should be distinguished as the most compassionate and most excellent servants in their fields. I return to this two-pronged theme when I discuss course grading—that I am called to honor God by evaluating my students with compassion and excellence; they immediately sense the relevance and complexities.

Of course, we should model our calling in our teaching. If we profess servant teaching, we also need to practice it with integrity. We are called to help our students learn in the various disciplines how to excellently and compassionately love God and our neighbors as ourselves. What a wonderful calling. We are blessed to be much more than just teachers.

When I tell my students on day one that for me teaching is a God-given calling, I add the following: "I believe you all are called to my class even if you have to take it as a requirement! Who knows what God has in store for us to learn along the way? Let's find out. What an honor!"

Reflection

How might seeking excellence and compassion help you pursue your calling as a servant teacher?

3

Begin Again

Decades ago, I was burned out. It was only weeks before a planned semester sabbatical that I'd been looking forward to. I had become disappointed in my university, my colleagues, and myself. I was deeply discouraged. I wondered why I was working so hard for students and a school that didn't seem to appreciate my efforts.

I didn't realize it at the time, but I was experiencing the arc of professional disenchantment. As Christian psychiatrist Paul Tournier puts it, we "began full of enthusiasm, treating [our] work as a fascinating adventure. And then gradually, imperceptibly, as a result of disappointments, through the deadening effect of routine, even without . . . realizing why, it became a burden, just a duty to be performed, a habit, a prison rather than an adventure."[15] My burden included anxiety and depression. Previously excited to be a Christian professor, I found myself caught in a downward spiral.

I also sensed that I was disappointing my students. I felt shame, especially when I read my course evaluations; in my overly sensitive emotional state, even just a handful of negative comments wounded me.

My semester off became a time of rest and reflection as well as study. I needed to put my life back together. I sought a psychiatrist and therapist. My new psychiatrist mentioned that most of his clients in higher education had been going through similar despondency. Knowing that I was not alone, and with professional help, I found extra courage to begin again.

During my much-needed sabbatical, I noted three things that have helped me considerably in subsequent years.

First, I realized that each year, semester, course, and class session is a time to begin again. We servant teachers can reflect on how we have done in the past and what we might do differently in the future. We can thank God for every good gain and recommit ourselves to moving ahead with greater faith, skill, and virtue. In this sense, the recurring rhythms of the academic calendar can be great blessings—almost like the church year with its opportunities for self-examination, recommitment, and renewal.

Second, I discovered that I was being too hard on myself. I was seeking earthly perfection rather than realistic excellence, thereby repeatedly disappointing myself in spite of my successes with particular students and courses. Bernard of Clairvaux said that biblical "perfection" actually "consists in doing common and everyday things in an uncommon manner, and not in doing great things, nor in doing many things."[16]

I realized that my disappointment would strike even before the start of each semester. I love sitting down with a cup of coffee and a blank pad of paper to begin planning a new course, from the topics to readings, and from lecture-discussions to projects and papers. As the semester approaches, however, my enthusiasm wanes. I feel the pressure of time, such as a semester or quarter with a limited number of class meetings or online discussion posts. I review possible textbooks and become discouraged because so many are both uninspiring and expensive. Some of the great ideas I had for student assignments suddenly seem like enormous grading burdens. To return to the biblical garden metaphor from chapter 2, I wonder how much student land I can actually till for the kingdom. I begin getting discouraged before I even begin again!

Third, I concluded that I need one or two colleagues with whom I can be fully transparent about the ups and downs of my servant teaching. In other words, I need the stability of love and acceptance amid the highs and lows of the academy. I am lost if I don't have the kind of professional community that transcends the arc of professional disenchantment. My church community is essential, but I also need faithful, loving colleagues who care about me.

We can mistakenly impose upon ourselves unrealistic expectations flowing from our genuine desire to love God and our students. But every time we begin again, we have the wonderful opportunity to pursue excellence within our means, with plenty of compassion toward ourselves.

The longer I am a servant teacher, the better I am at fending off the arc of professional disenchantment by beginning each initiative—every year, term, and class meeting—with realistic expectations. Then I have the emotional-spiritual as well as professional resources to do common and everyday things in an uncommon manner, God helping me.

Reflection

Where do you find yourself along the arc of professional disenchantment—and how might you begin again?

4

Name Names

For years, the first session of a new class always burdened me. I wanted to get us all off to a good start, but I felt very anxious about the new relationships between my students and me, and among my students. So I sought a better, more organic, and less stressful way of forming a new learning community each term.

I began by emailing students in advance and asking them their preferred first names. I wanted to let them know that even though I might not have met them personally, they belonged to our inchoate class community.

That simple practice morphed into an unusual way of nurturing community. In at least my smaller classes, I send students an optional precourse questionnaire to find out more about each of them, including how I might serve them (for the sake of privacy, students can opt out of answering any of the questions, but few do).

About a week before class begins, I distribute via email a questionnaire that students can fill in and return to help me get to know them, their possible interest in course topics, their learning styles, and the like. I also ask them their major(s) and minor(s). What would they like to be doing after college? Are there ways that I can help them learn (see the appendix)?

In short, I ask them about who they are and how I can best serve them. I then begin relating to them as persons. I keep the completed questionnaires and often refer to them before meeting with individual students, and even before writing my final comments on a student assignment—just to remind myself of my personal audience.

In the biblical tradition, "naming" is about knowing. To name something is to identify it for what it is, not what we think it is. Naming and knowing are "intimate" actions in the Hebrew sense of *yada'* (e.g., Jer. 16:21; Ezek. 30:8). When we recognize our students' preferred names, we acknowledge them as distinct individuals with their own meaningful lives. We invite them personally into community. And we teach in Jesus' name, accepting His invitation to be educational ambassadors to our God-known students.

In appropriate classes, my precourse questionnaire carries me across the first-day borderlands between impersonal and personal teaching, from isolated teacher and student to emerging community. I respond to each completed questionnaire with a short, personal note of thanks and an indication about how I might serve the student based on their learning needs/styles and topical interests related to the course. I bring blank paper copies of the questionnaire to class for newcomers not listed on the earlier roster, asking them to fill out the form during the first class session.

Once I began this precourse practice, I discovered that even on day one many students were primed for classroom discussion. By connecting with them personally, I had told them that they matter, that they are known and belong. When calling on them while reviewing the roster on the first day, I use their preferred name; I don't have to ask for it perfunctorily.

Also on day one, I introduce myself by name and appropriate titles (e.g., Dr., Mr., or Professor), briefly describe my faith journey, review a few of my teaching strengths and weaknesses, and explain how I got the name "Quentin" (as Latin, for the fifth one in the family). I essentially answer the student questionnaire myself, for my students.

The power of naming ourselves—of personal transparency—is significant in teaching already on day one. When students connect with us affectively, they sense that their learning has meaning. They wish to perform well because they rightly feel that their instructor cares about them personally.

A few years after I demonstrated this transparency in a course lecture at a Southern evangelical university, a female professor who attended wrote to me, "Hearing your lecture had a profound impact on me. It demonstrated how vulnerability creates an instant connection with students. . . . Now my course evaluations . . . are almost perfect."

I always address students by name in my email and text messages. The simple practice reminds me to communicate personally and to craft my words carefully. I am communicating with a God-known person, not just a student. And I sign each message with my full name. I carry this through in my grading, using the student's and my name with my comments. I name names, in Jesus' name.

Reflection

How might you get to know your students enough to serve them personally—and how can they get to know you?

5

Respect Learners

On the first day of class I tell students that we'll learn and grow together throughout the term. I add that we'll probably fail sometimes. But we'll do the best we can, encouraging each other through the ups and downs.

Then I say something like this: "I want you to know that I will never look down on you as a person based on your academic performance. We all have many things going on in our lives, some of which might be more important than this course. If you have significant life challenges, please attend to them, knowing that I care and will not judge you for it." I repeat the same words when I return the first round of graded assignments.

In both cases, I make it clear that they do not have to share their personal life struggles with me and that I can't always adjust their grades simply because of such challenges—although I have done so, such as when a student's roommate tried to commit suicide, when a student lost a parent to cancer, when a student suffered an attempted rape, and when a student was fired from an excellent job for rejecting her supervisor's advances. Then there are the more common setbacks like illnesses and, increasingly, students'

45

anxiety and depression. Students howled when I told them that my fox terrier ate their papers. We all are dealing with life challenges during our teaching and learning.

We servant teachers work in a difficult context where self-worth is often tied to worldly status, including grades, degrees, academic majors, and job titles. Academic cultures create and sustain their own pecking orders that can discount life and personal experience. I know this firsthand.

I grew up with an alcoholic father who died when I was in high school. My mother, a paranoid schizophrenic, was unable to get a driver's license let alone give me love and support. I have suffered from lifelong depression and anxiety. Sometimes I still feel like an imposter in front of students.

Moreover, I grew up hating school. School fueled my insecurities. I never attended a high school social event, played sports, acted, or debated. Practically no one at school knew me. No one invited me to get together with them—and I would not invite friends to my house because of my embarrassing living conditions. I was a loner who felt like a loser.

I discovered in my journey toward servant teaching that God uses our brokenness as well as our gifts. For instance, I realized that God was using my own emotional wounds to help me connect with students. So when I tell my students that I will never judge them as human beings based on their academic performance, I describe the time my high school Spanish teacher asked me to stand up and recite something from memory. Unprepared, as usual, I stood in silence. She shook her head sadly and said, "Oh, Pedro [the name she gave me], what are we going to do with you?" Studying was a low priority for me. I was trying to survive with my mentally ill mother, living in a trailer with barely enough money for food.

When I tell the Pedro story in class, I receive grateful notes from struggling students. I respond that I am thankful they are in my course. Many students today are hurting; anxiety and depression are common. Learners desire warmly empathetic instructors. I aim to be one, partly by respecting myself as well as my students, and celebrating what God does through me, also a learner.

One practice I have found particularly helpful for respecting my students is addressing them either as "colleagues" or as professional practitioners of the course subject. For instance, I call students in my media criticism course "media critics"; my emails to them begin, "Dear media critics." Since I teach public speaking from the Augustinian perspective of "servant speaking" (loving one's audience as one's neighbors), I address those students as "servant speakers."

If we treat students in ways that suggest they are merely immature, irresponsible, and dependent persons, we actually contribute to students seeing themselves through such lenses. At the same time, we set up an us-versus-them mentality that reduces our capacity for empathy and might even decrease their academic motivation. After all, we too are learners; students teach us many things, including how best to serve them.

The Pedro story is simply one way of reminding my students and myself that we need to respect each other as we wish to be respected—and as God respects us. Just like our students, we go through different periods in life. Our personal struggles affect how we teach, just as students' difficulties affect their learning. Yet we grow and learn together, respecting one another as brothers and sisters in Christ. We view and treat one another as God's precious children.

Reflection

What practices might you use to convey your wholehearted respect for your students as God's image bearers?

6

Welcome Doubters

The North American church is losing younger members. College is a critical time for forming or rejecting faith, but religious disenchantment grows already during middle and high school. As college educators, we inherit the results.

I have struggled with this issue partly because I want to ensure that my students have heard the love-drenched gospel of Jesus Christ. Also, I know from conversations with students at many Christian universities that they often see the church as hypocritical, unloving, and culturally backward.

Therefore, on the first day of class, and later as appropriate, I share a bit of my faith journey—after talking about my own academic path and my family life. I realize that I am not my students' pastor, and I teach in a classroom or online, not in a church. Still, my students and I are at an avowedly Christian university where faith is relevant to our relationships as well as to the subjects we study.

I hope to offer a winsome, transparent testimony with space for doubting students to feel welcome. Then I can comfortably call upon my faith journey as appropriate during the course, including when students express their concerns about the church in class sessions or in private conversations.

I begin by saying something like this: "I just want you to know that although we are together at a Christian university, we might be at different places in our faith journeys. It can be confusing. Even the word 'Christian' means so many different things to people. For some, it connotes specific political or moral convictions. For others, it means rules and regulations and even hypocrisy. I get it. I have some of those feelings too."

I continue, "You will hear me talking about being a 'follower of Jesus Christ' because that's how I view myself. To me, being a Christian means following Jesus. I'll invite you during the semester to follow Jesus as well—maybe when I talk about discerning a Christian perspective on our course topics. The Bible is especially important, but we have to be careful not to misuse Scripture."

Finally, I know from experience that I need to say something specifically about doubt. Many of my students carry doubts; some of them have significant doubts about Jesus or at least the institutional church, even if they don't admit their doubt to others. Some students are quiet skeptics.

I say, "Maybe some of you have doubt about following Jesus. I get that too. In fact, I have doubts, especially when terrible things happen. I struggle to understand why God let me grow up in a difficult family situation that contributed to my lifelong anxiety and depression. I struggle when I see how some Christians and churches treat people, and when some apparent Jesus followers say awful things about others in public.

"But then I think about the blessed person who wrote the book of Hebrews near the end of the Bible. The writer talks about great people of faith, including Abraham, the father of the Jews. The author says that Abraham went forward in faith even though he didn't know where he was going [Heb. 11:8]. Wow, that's me too. I follow Jesus, but often I don't know how to be faithful in today's crazy world. So if you too have doubts, if you feel lost sometimes, I am so glad you're here. We'll journey together."

I never want to challenge students' faith in ways that will turn them away from the Lord, causing them to "stumble" (Rom. 14:13–23). But I do seek to be honest and transparent so students trust me and feel free to talk with me privately about their faith and their doubts.

This also provides a context for me to assure students that although I am deeply committed to a "Christian perspective" in my field of communication, there are different views from within the faith. I want to hear about their journeys to be faithful communicators in a broken world. I certainly don't want to create the impression that I have all of the answers. In short, I hope to welcome doubters to a lifelong journey of following Jesus Christ, with all of its joys and perplexities.

I am convinced that our approach to doubters is enormously important for the future of Christian higher education. If we can model authentic, humble faith, we will teach through powerful attraction; we will persuade by demonstrating authentic faith in action, doubts and all.

Reflection

How might you address religious doubt in ways that affirm students on the journey, especially in your discipline?

7

Pray Humbly

I begin every class with a traditional Christian greeting and response. I say, "The Lord be with you." The students respond, "And also with you." I explain that I wish to establish the right context each time we convene—namely, that we are a community seeking God's blessing for each other as we teach and learn together. In my experience, this is a fitting way to begin every class; students tell me they appreciate it.

I learned, however, that I first need to prepare my heart and gain students' attention. I wait for the students to settle down. Once everyone is quiet and looking at me, I make eye contact with students from one side of the classroom to the other. Finally, I wait a few more seconds and sincerely ask God to be with my students for our time together—"The Lord be with you." When I do all of this, the student response seems genuine. Sometimes, after the students respond, I add, "Thank you" or "Amen." We use this simple litany as a prayer for remembering who and whose we are as teacher and students.

It seems to me that how and when we pray with students for the sake of nurturing a Christian learning community should fit naturally with our teaching styles and private student interactions. In my view, there is no correct practice. Yet prayer is essential for servant teaching.

I always pray with students at the beginning of class on the days we return from breaks, to bring us back together before the face of God. I thank the Lord for keeping us safe. I also pray at the end of class before students depart for breaks. I pray for traveling mercies. I pray that we'll remember each other during our time apart. And I pray that students' interactions with family and friends during breaks will be a blessing even if challenging. Finally, I always pray with students when there is a local, national, or international tragedy. The most difficult times for me have been when a student passed away unexpectedly because of an accident or suicide. The event is on everyone's mind, and to ignore it seems uncaring.

I don't normally tell my students, but I pray for them regularly. I use my class roster or a sheet of student photos to identify each one. I find that such prayer keeps my heart open to students. It helps me follow through on my promise never to evaluate them as human beings based on their academic performance (see chapter 5).

During much of my professorial life, I focused my private prayers as petitions, asking God to bless my students, colleagues, and me for the educational needs of the day. Today, I focus even more on simply giving thanks for the opportunity to serve students. I thank God for each of them. I thank God for every bit of learning that takes place, including the learning beyond what I will ever witness personally—the learning beyond tests, exams, and papers that happens within students and sometimes even transforms their lives. This kind of doxological prayer opens my heart and mind for the sake of loving my students as brothers and sisters in Christ.

Another form of servant-teaching prayer I find essential is maintaining a sense of God's presence. For me, this is ongoing dialogue with God, prompted and maintained by the Holy Spirit.

I appreciate what Dietrich Bonhoeffer says about such prayer in his book on Christian community, *Life Together*. Using Psalm 119 as an example, he suggests that "prayer is not a matter of pouring out the human heart once and for all in need or joy, but an unbroken, constant learning, accepting, and impressing [upon our minds of] God's will in Jesus Christ."[17] Such prayer is a way of reminding ourselves as servant teachers that we can't separate the knowledge of ourselves from the knowledge of God; we are called to think and act in tune with God's wisdom as revealed in Scripture.

To put it differently, all of our teaching and learning are essentially prayerful acts of "faith seeking understanding."[18] We learn to pray, and pray to learn.

My private prayers about my teaching naturally integrate with course preparation. I think and pray. I rehearse in my mind what I will say to students, knowing that God is with me, wishing me to serve students well. As Henri Nouwen puts it, my thoughtful planning becomes unceasing prayer (1 Thess. 5:17).[19]

In a sense, I prayerfully aim as a servant teacher to engage my mind humbly through my open heart rather than through my self-controlling ego.[20] This seems like right and fitting prayer for servant teaching.

Reflection

How does or should prayer guide your life as a servant teacher?

8

Select Engaging Texts

Thomas Merton recalls the story of a philosopher asking the desert father St. Anthony how Anthony could be happy when he was "deprived of the consolation of books." Anthony replied, "My book, O philosopher, is the nature of created things, and any time I want to read the words of God, the book is before me."[21]

So do we need textbooks? Why not just study all of creation directly? The answer, of course, is that many people already have studied God's world, leading the way with encapsulated knowledge for us to use, enjoy, and discerningly pass along.

But students greatly dislike "boring" and "expensive" textbooks. Students at one school told me that their communication texts are so dull that they buy one text to make copies of the chapter summaries to pass around before quizzes and exams. I wonder: How can a book about human communication be so dull? What would the desert fathers make of today's textbooks on human communication?

Let's assume that it's difficult to write a student-engaging textbook. Let's also assume that our students grow up not liking textbooks—just as they are socialized to complain about campus cafeteria food.

Fortunately, we have the freedom to evaluate the books we use from the perspectives of our students, not just based on our knowledge of a discipline or authors. Will students like a particular book—at least more than others? Will they be inclined to read it? Must we use reading quizzes to get them to crack it open?

Of course, particular subjects and courses will inevitably be less interesting to some students. Yet we always have choices among texts unless our campus administrators lock us into contracts with e-book publishers or we must use the same text as the colleagues who are teaching the course. In any case, why not seek student input when selecting texts?

I find that if I ask even just three students to rank three different texts, I can make a better choice. I ask them individually to fill out a short form telling me what they like and don't like about each text, along with a ranking. Student reviewers are susceptible to group think, so I don't have them evaluate texts together. I tell them the used and new prices for each text and e-book.

At first, I thought students would simply select the shorter book with the most graphics. But students seem to be more interested in whether the prose is engaging and the material is well organized, not the graphics per se. They prefer a book with more space on the page, not text jammed together. Also, they like clear chapter previews, outlines, and summaries. Finally, they prefer fewer chapters overall as long as each chapter is not too long. My communication-text findings might not be representative of all disciplines, but they suggest that students are not well served by some of our textbook choices.

I have written a few academic books used as textbooks. I tested manuscript drafts with entire classes before final editing. This, too, gave me a sense of what makes for a good textbook: student-oriented examples and illustrations, shorter chapters, clear organization, and the author's personal voice. I have thoroughly rewritten and even eliminated chapters based on student feedback.

What if we already have prepared lectures and ancillary material for use with an existing textbook? I still think it's worth reconsidering our text choice every few years. If we find one that students vastly prefer, they will be more motivated to read it. Also, we might discover better ways of teaching as we interact with freshly formulated material.

Another possibility for some courses is using academic trade books instead of textbooks. They are less expensive as well as more thoughtful and engaging. These are the books that most shaped my understanding of faith and communication over the years, so I am partial to them. Yet I find it easier just to assign a textbook rather than try to integrate several trade books into a course. The older I get, however, the more inclined I am to use trade books that I know will engage students. Students appreciate it, often telling me that they are glad to read the books.

As a servant teacher, I remain restless about textbook selections. I wonder if there is a better way. I wonder if more of us should be writing books, making our disciplines come alive by prompting students' wonder and delight. St. Anthony was right about the importance of studying (and appreciating) God's world directly. But well-written books can direct students to an everyday appreciation of God's world as well.

Reflection
How might you select the "best" texts for serving students?

9

Eliminate Busywork

In the previous chapter I complained about the boring and expensive textbooks that we assign either because we wrongly assume they serve the students well or because we don't have viable alternatives. I mentioned that students complain to me about textbooks.

But an even greater student complaint is what they call "busywork." The vast majority of students feel that much of their academic effort is a waste of time. They see themselves doing it because they must in order to get the academic credit to get a college degree to get a job. Even at the college level, many feel trapped in the same kind of educational system they have tolerated for all of their preuniversity instruction. To some of them, much of their academic work is mere "schooling"; they learn material to regurgitate it on exams.

As for faculty, four decades in higher education taught me that educators like doing more and requiring others to do more. I attended faculty meetings dutifully, witnessing how committees begat committees, syllabi created more and longer syllabi, requirements produced yet more requirements, assessors devised even more assessments, curricula generated additional curricula, and so on. I don't recall ever witnessing faculty reduce the requirements for a course revision except when the administration or an accrediting agency mandated it. We faculty make ourselves and our students ever busier, and then complain about our busyness.

At the same time, the purposes of our professorial busyness can evaporate over time. We live in a world of creeping activities seemingly disconnected from their original purposes. I like Søren Kierkegaard's metaphor: We are "panting on our activistic errands. But we are not running on the racetrack."[22] We even lose track of the essentials.

Those of us in Christian higher education generally work hard out of a sense of duty to God and community. We tend to be sincere, selfless people. We emphasize great teaching, which requires considerable work. Many of us feel guilty when we are not working at our utmost for God's glory. Along the way, we forget that our work is to be a form of worship (see chapter 2) and that worship requires a spirit of Sabbath rest (Gen. 2:2–3, 15), in which we remember and contemplate what *God* is accomplishing.

How much of what we do is truly essential and contributes to students' long-term growth? Should we really be doing everything we are doing? Or do we fall into the same problem that our students are complaining about behind our backs—namely, busywork? Dare I ask this: Is the Christian academic system obsessed with busyness as a kind of restless, even self-righteous enterprise?

We tend to think about course content in terms of our academic disciplines or even our research specialties. This is not all bad, as I explain in chapter 11 on teaching information-rich courses. Suppose, instead, we imagine most courses as essentially "core" courses, designed to teach the basics of what students should know, particularly material that will help them in life. These courses could emphasize ideas or skills, or both.

For instance, when I teach public speaking, I focus on the essentials, not on all of the material covered in over-written textbooks. I emphasize principles that students can practice repeatedly in my and other classes. If I think about a public speaking course as a means of serving students rather than covering abundant material, I can make it more interesting and beneficial. This basic approach helps nurture classroom community as well as individual student success. Students have time to grow together in both knowledge and skill—and they like and appreciate it.

One school I worked at sent a questionnaire to recent graduates, asking them to briefly describe the "Christian worldview" they learned at the university. Most students never responded even after a reminder. Those who did respond couldn't articulate even the basics of a coherent Christian worldview. How can that happen?

My guess is that students retain at most 20 percent of what they learn during their college career, even just a few months after graduating. Of course, they also learn essential practices such as writing clearly, thinking well, engaging in civil discourse, and being faithful. These are the kinds of curricular and course goals that we shouldn't overlook. But we need to discern what we and our students consider busywork versus what actually is busywork; then we can minimize the real busywork, saving our students' and our own time in the long run. Moreover, we should then be able to help students formulate and use a coherent Christian worldview.

Reflection

How might you decide what is essential and what is mere busywork in your courses?

10

Do Less with Less

Early in my teaching career, I saw my busyness as a sign of God's blessing. Today, I still favor a strong work ethic, but not at the expense of my overall health. As a servant teacher, I hold that we can't be all things to all students in all situations in order to make everything right in the world. We have to make tough decisions about our limited resources because there never will be enough time to do everything we think should be done. We always face trade-offs.

Over the years, I have repeatedly had to say "no" to myself about nonstop bustle, thereby teaching less material but with greater and more lasting student learning. I've had to give up unrealistic expectations, thereby doing less with less, but doing it more effectively and with greater Sabbath rest along the way.

As Henri Nouwen says, productivity and success can greatly enhance our lives, "but when our value as human beings depends on what we make with our hands and minds, we become victims of the fear tactics of our world." He adds that when productivity becomes our way of "overcoming self-doubt, we are extremely vulnerable to rejection and criticism and prone to inner anxiety and depression."[23] Yet excessive busyness itself continues to give us the impression that we are earning our keep as Christian teacher-scholars. After all, we are doing kingdom work!

God is with us, calling us to stop fearing and to slow down because his burden is light (Matt. 11:28–30). We can witness over time that doing less bears new kinds of fruit for us and our students—even for the health of our educational communities. Eugene H. Peterson writes, "In any creative enterprise there are risks, mistakes, false starts, failures, frustrations, embarrassments, but out of this mess—when we stay with it long enough, enter it deeply enough—there slowly emerges love or beauty or peace."[24] To teach and learn in such a place of love, beauty, and peace is a grand blessing. We then teach for life, not just for immediate academic performance.

An academic administrator told one of my colleagues "to do more with less." It's a common refrain, suggesting we all need to work harder because, after all, these are "difficult times." There is some truth to it. Generally speaking, we have larger classes, more programs, more ill-prepared students, more nonteaching duties, and fewer resources. Many of us have to teach both in classrooms and online. It's exhausting.

But another way of looking at our situation is that we should be doing less with fewer resources. We should focus well on the essentials so we can instruct patiently with excellence and compassion.

I believe that we might need to reduce the pace of our work and student learning. Then we can rediscover what

Peterson calls the love, beauty, and peace in our everyday interactions, both in and out of the classroom, with administrators and support staff as well as students. We should do this not just because we will live longer and happier lives, but even more because the gospel doesn't require us to complete our own perfection, but instead to depend more on God and less on ourselves. Our work should be smart, student focused, and community nurturing. Less frenzy can foster richer, more lasting, life-changing learning.

One of my mentors told me that I was lazy and arrogant. He said that I was too lazy to set priorities and stick with them; I was flying every which way at the same time. Ideas and activities swirled around me like the dirt around Pigpen in the *Peanuts* comics. After he said this to me, in love, I realized that I was always hustling across campus; I rarely walked at a normal pace. My physical pace echoed my mental condition. What I saw as God-pleasing busyness was also a kind of personal chaos.

Moreover, he said I was arrogant. I had no problem with that characterization. Thinking more highly of others and less highly of myself has never come easily to me. I even wonder now if this book is partly an attempt to showcase my pedagogical superiority.

But my mentor meant something else: I was arrogant in the sense that I thought I had to be the one to accomplish things correctly. Why let a student give a mediocre presentation when I could give a better one? Why let God do His work through students when I can do it better? Doesn't God need *me*? What could he accomplish without me?

Doing less with less is the freedom to focus on what most matters, with one another and God. Modeling this for students is a blessing for our educational communities. And it helps us cultivate Sabbath rest for our souls even as we labor under the Lord's easy yoke.

Reflection

How might you better serve students (and yourself) by doing less with less?

11

Outline Info-Rich Courses

I suggested previously that both busywork and our compulsion to do more with less can hinder our success as servant teachers. Nevertheless, there are information-rich (info-rich) courses that require covering a lot of material. How can we serve students well in such courses?

Frequently the place of info-rich courses in the curriculum gives us few options for reducing student requirements or our grading load. For students going to graduate school in the natural sciences, for example, there is considerable material to cover. Also, advanced courses within a discipline might have to include copious information.

When I teach an info-rich course, I try to make it as straightforward and predictable as possible. I assume that students and I will be busy and stressed out along the way. Learners might get behind in the course as they also attend to the rest of their academics along with extracurricular activities, some of which might be essential for their emotional health.

I desire to teach in ways that will help students stay on track and up to date. I aim to clarify the learning process rather than reduce the necessary course content or requirements. Organization is key.

I give students an extended outline (7–10 pages) with the syllabus, summarizing what students need to learn in the course. It lists topics and the related page numbers from the text. I say, "This is what we will cover. Everything I'll ask you about on exams is listed on this outline. If you can answer questions about this material, you'll do splendidly in the course. Moreover, I'll cover these topics one by one, in order, referring to text material. If you read the text in advance and relate it to the outline, you'll be able to follow really well."

When I begin each session, I remind students where we are on the outline and highlight what we hope to cover that day. I encourage learners to check off each item on the outline as we cover it. That way, if someone is absent they know exactly what they missed.

I add, "I encourage you to make notes in the text as I refer to textbook pages during class. Always bring your notebook or laptop and text to class." I further say, "If I am not going to cover a topic that's on the outline, usually because I am short on time, I'll point you to that section of the text so you can study it on your own or in groups." I explain that my goal is to avoid making the course seem like a stressful game in which I am trying to catch the students for not knowing something that they didn't even know would be covered in the course.

Of course, I still need to make every class as interesting and memorable as possible to hold students' attention and keep them motivated. But I must keep my examples and illustrations under control; I tend to overdo them, both the quantity and length.

Sometimes I use reading quizzes to encourage learners to keep up in the text. I normally give eleven quizzes randomly over the term and eliminate the lowest grade (everyone has a bad day). I motivate students by telling them that I will select some exam questions directly from the quiz questions, word for word, and we will briefly review each quiz when I return it at the following class session. Students use their copies of quizzes as part of their study guide for exams.

I always schedule exam-preparation review sessions for info-rich courses, even if I have to use regular class meeting periods because students are not available at other times. I send students an email the day before the review just to remind them that they might want to read through the outline and prepare questions in advance as preparation for both the review and the exam.

At the review sessions, I use the outline to make a few points about each item and to ask for questions related to each one. Occasionally we run out of time during a review session, so I then schedule a follow-up session, often for later the same day. Since not all students will be able to attend, I record the follow-up session and distribute the recording by email immediately afterward. If I will be using visuals in the review, I video record the review session as well.

My view of teaching an info-rich course changed over the years as I pursued servant teaching. I want students to do well, so I share the burden with them. I put more time into course planning and organization—especially the first time I teach it—so learners can identify precisely what they should know. Since I have limited class time, I depend more on the carefully selected textbook, always helping students relate text topics to the outline and my class presentations.

Reflection

How might you teach info-rich courses to maximize student learning and minimize your and students' stress?

12

Create Covenantal Syllabi

My syllabi include two points about tardiness. First, students should make every effort to come to class no matter how late. We will have available seats for them by the door so they can slip in with minimal disruption (I ask for two volunteers to make sure the seats are saved each session throughout the term). I explain that being tardy is far better than not showing up. I use the example of being late for a date. Would it ever be better not to show up at all?

My second point about tardiness says that students should call or text me if I am late. I give them my cell number, just as I ask them for theirs in my precourse questionnaire (see the appendix). When I review this point in class, I ask students to imagine that I was in an accident or had a flat tire and was running late. I tell them that once the department assistant came to my office to ask if I was supposed to be in class. I dashed to the classroom about ten minutes late. Most of the students had already left, based on a mythical ten-minute rule. If only a student had called me!

One of my goals with a syllabus is to capture covenantal practices for mutual responsibility and care. I want students to know specifically what's required of them. But I also want them to know what's required of me (e.g., I promise to return all submitted, on-time class materials within two class sessions—one class session if it is a weekly course).[25] For me, a syllabus is not a one-way legal document indicating what students must perform and the consequences if they don't. It's more of a description of community practices with mutual understandings as well as obligations.

I send my proposed syllabus to students a week in advance of the course in order to solicit feedback for our syllabus discussion on the first day of class (with paper copies for students who add the course at the last minute). I have the final say, but I hope we can come to agreement on both technical fine points and the spirit behind the syllabus.

I hope to answer these questions: Will the syllabus help us to function as a community? Will my approach to testing and grading reduce anxiety and enhance learning? Are there better alternatives? What about the schedule, given everything else happening on campus during the key dates for exams and submissions? How should we help a classmate who must miss one or more sessions? Would someone be willing to audio record class sessions for absent students or those who wish to relisten? Should students encourage one another to share lecture or reading notes, or even to form study groups?

Not all students will read the syllabus in advance. Some of them doubt that their input matters. Still, I want my students to know that the syllabus is a communal document worth reading and revising together before we begin the term—and then reviewing key points during the term.

I rarely make significant changes after we have settled on the syllabus and the course has begun. In my experience, students deeply dislike such changes. Schedule alterations, in particular, frustrate some students; for such changes, I require 100 percent student agreement via an anonymous ballot. Otherwise, if I just discuss the issue openly with the entire class, the sheepish students will go along with the crowd even if they would face serious schedule conflicts.

I clarify in my syllabi the "penalty" for late assignments—usually one grade per day, assuming a student doesn't have a justification. Students can have legitimate reasons for submitting material late, but I don't want to encourage them to do last-minute work, which is usually inferior and leads to a lower grade anyway. I want to encourage them to work ahead, toward excellence, if at all possible. The sooner they let me know they can't meet a deadline, the better. Once I hear about their situation, we can negotiate an alternative deadline, although I might require them to submit preliminary work before the new deadline to keep them on the new schedule.

I think there are essentially two ways of framing a syllabus—as a kind of legal document or as a type of "rule for living," like the community guidelines of ancient monasteries. In Western, litigious societies, syllabi increasingly resemble legal documents. Although this is understandable, I am concerned about what our syllabi communicate. How do students feel about them? How do we feel about them? Do our syllabi capture the importance of love, service, and community? Do they reflect our God-given vocation to serve one another with excellence and compassion? Do they encourage and guide us as servant teachers as well as guide our students to community? In short, can syllabi help us all to be our best selves in community?

Reflection
How might your syllabi embrace covenantal community rather than just legalism?

13

Forestall Cheating

In my early days of Christian university teaching, I naively assumed that students wouldn't cheat. Then I found out about students in one section of my course sharing information about the exam that I would also be giving later that day to a second section. A student told me what was happening, concerned that the cheating would lower his grade on the curve even though he didn't accept the exam information offered by a friend. I agreed with my student that cheating is unfair as well as unethical.

I decided that I should make it difficult for students to be academically dishonest. I don't want to tempt them. Also, I don't want to get into a cat-and-mouse game with students over dishonesty. I dislike hunting for evidence of cheating, such as using websites to compare submitted student papers with those for sale online. The idea of thinking about my students as cheaters darkens my view of them as God's image bearers preparing for service in his world.

The exam problem was easy to fix: I began giving separate exams to each course section as well as changing the exams from term to term, with only a few carryover questions. I also started giving copies of past exams to students to prepare for future ones, telling them that the samples would help them understand how I write exams, not provide all the specific questions for future exams.[26]

Interestingly, providing previous exams actually motivated many students to form small groups to work together on studying for my exams. Also, students would bring up questions from past exams when I conducted reviews for upcoming exams. I realized that my solution to the exam cheating problem was a student learning incentive.

What about papers, especially essays? As I see the problem, there are essentially two forms of cheating to address: unattributed material "borrowed" from online or other sources (including just ideas or theses), and entire papers, purchased online.

I eventually concluded that I couldn't monitor the borrowing of ideas, so I turned the problem on its head as a benefit to learners. I encourage students to borrow ideas by attributing the ideas to respected sources. In other words, I ask students to determine the best sources for their essay topics and to make it clear exactly what and whose material they have used, providing necessary citations. I do this even when I teach an applied course like public speaking; students must cite in their outlines and actual speeches at least one academic and two popular sources. I explain in the syllabus what such sources are and how to find them—with a librarian's contact information for additional help.

Buying or borrowing entire papers is such a significant ethical issue that I couldn't believe that Christian students would ever think it was justified. I was wrong. In my experience, however, the few who attempt this tend to be students who procrastinate and then violate their own consciences. They feel like it's the only way out of a self-created jam. Then they submit a paper that is too general—and often too well written to be composed specifically for my course by the particular student.

Two practices work for me. First, I require students to submit ideas and outlines in advance. I aim to discourage procrastination. Also, the early feedback catches problems with ill-conceived essays so the students get on a productive track and I can avoid a lot of explanatory grading when the paper is finally submitted.

Second, I create essay rubrics that require writers to use my own, course-specific concepts that are not available in generic forms elsewhere. Usually this involves terms I create for each course—like "servant teaching" in this book. I tell the students—and put in the syllabus—that the essay has to show me that it's course specific and includes course-specific language even in the thesis itself.

I may also require that students use concepts specifically related to how we are integrating faith and learning in the course; that alone guarantees that students won't purchase an essay from one of the online sellers. In both types of course-specific requirements, I am able to catch problems early on with student-submitted ideas and outlines. My approaches not only work; they improve student performance in tune with faith-based ethics.

I hope to forestall cheating—to make it more difficult and thereby to discourage it. I look for course-specific assignments that are not generic and that will require students to focus on class material.

Reflection

How might you address academic dishonesty as a servant teacher in your discipline?

14

Foster Applied Learning

When students see how my courses will equip them to serve others, they are more grateful and motivated. I find this to be especially true for the kinds of assignments I give students as well as for service credit (see chapter 22). Whenever appropriate, I create assignments that provide students with opportunities to serve others in a class, school, church, or the wider community.

I see this as an essential role for me as a servant teacher committed to the holistic growth of learners. I also see it as important for helping students to avoid a "schooling" attitude (merely learning information temporarily for exams and grades) and to find biblical purpose in their academics (specifically, caretaking with excellence and compassion, chapter 2).

For example, in order to help my students understand how organizational documents can grow stale, I asked them to critique the campus document covering student behavior: What works well in the document? What seems juvenile? Is anything hypocritical? Which rules or regulations are many students already violating—perhaps without staff oversight, let alone penalty? What missing items should be included? Are the principles truly biblical?

Then we invited the student life administrators to our class to hear ideas for improving their document. The administrators were impressed; they agreed to review the document and make recommendations to university leadership, all designed to create a clearer and more relevant set of covenantal expectations.

As I mentioned earlier, I teach public speaking as "servant speaking." Instead of having students give the usual speeches on popular topics, I ask them to identify on-campus audiences and deliver speeches that serve those audiences. Then we invite representatives of each audience to class to hear the related speeches. The speeches have led to changes in campus policies, procedures, and even landscaping. Students see what a difference it makes to approach their learning as service to others, in tune with their biblical calling to be caretakers of God's world.

During my academic program reviews at different universities, I advise schools to accept full academic credit for at least two internships. Yet I know that an internship without specific goals shared by the student and sponsor is less valuable. I ask each intern to meet with the sponsor to come up with a list of ways that the student can serve the organization. Then I review that list with the student in order to determine which of those items is most important for the student's learning—usually by ranking them and selecting the top three. I explain to the student and the sponsor that the student will be evaluated according to how well he or she progresses on those items.

I find that intern journaling is essential for three reasons. First, the student needs to document both the learning and the reflection on that learning. This provides a "text" for me to use in discussing with the student their progress toward internship goals.

Second, journaling gets the student to record the learning for later résumé writing and job interviewing. I hope the journaling helps some students to become more reflective about their lives apart from the internship. I ask them what they are learning that will help them serve others after the internship.

Finally, journaling helps me assess how well the sponsor is contributing to the learning goals for the student. If the student rarely mentions the sponsor, I know there's a problem I'll have to address, usually by discussing the situation with the sponsor, preferably at the workplace in case we need to include others in the conversation.

I fully support the popular practices of "service" and "experiential" learning. But to be effective, they require a fair amount of administration by faculty or other staff, particularly for academic credit. Student assessment and self-reflection are critically important. I don't think formal service-learning experiences should be separate from the rest of the curriculum, but instead integrated across the curriculum.

Dietrich Bonhoeffer wrote in a letter from prison, "We must allow for the fact that most people learn wisdom only by personal experiences."[27] He served both inmates and guards while he was incarcerated, up to his execution. I gain more wisdom every time I read his books, including his letters from prison. I believe that teaching and learning through personal service are central to the experiential mission of a Christian university. We all learn partly by doing and reflecting in the service of others, not just by studying on our own.

Reflection

How might you use "applied" or "service" learning to promote learning in your courses?

15

Leverage Locale

In the previous chapter I advocated for across-the-curriculum applied learning. Now I would like to suggest that we should help students see that their education can equip them to serve God in specific locales, such as nearby neighborhood groups, businesses, and nonprofit organizations, including churches. Students thereby gain greater self-confidence as stewards of God's diverse world, stepping out of their generational and cultural comfort zones. And they capture a vision for how they might serve a community when they reside in one after college.

It seems to me that we best serve church and society when we give our students a vision for planting themselves in geographic communities. Augustine wrote, "All people should be loved equally. But you cannot do good to all people equally, so you should take particular thought for those who, as if by lot, happened to be particularly close to you in terms of place, time, or any other circumstances."[28] Many of our campuses are near areas of social and spiritual needs, fertile grounds for student action.

Partly because of peer-oriented social media, students tend to participate only superficially in geographic and cross-generational communities. Also, as Wendell Berry writes, some "schools are no longer oriented to a cultural inheritance that it is their duty to pass on unimpaired, but to the career, which is to say the future, of the child." He adds that a student is "educated to *leave* home and earn money in a provisional future that has nothing to do with place or community" (italics in original).[29] Without being nostalgic about where we and our students were raised, we can affirm the pedagogical importance of nurturing community-based learning to show how students, even in a digital world, might live and work faithfully in a particular place.

I fear that unless we embed our teaching in some of the different groups and cultures of our locales, we will fail to help our students catch a vision for becoming lifelong stewards of God's world. We tend to think of diversity according to categories—especially skin color and ethnicities—that run across geographic space. Consequently, we might overlook situated diversities in our own backyards.

Do we consider nearby locales as places and people for service? If not, our students can become local tourists, merely passing through neighborhoods contiguous to campus. Perhaps this is one of the reasons for students' loss of faith even while attending a Christian university; students become strangers to churches as local, cross-generational communities.

Do our students, rightly seeking new life experiences and an educational community, nevertheless become estranged from their own cultural roots? In an essay on the stranger in the Bible, Holocaust survivor Elie Wiesel addresses the issue of becoming a homeless native. He says the stranger, who leaves behind home and culture, might understandably feel a "need to renew, . . . to replenish." The stranger "may leave his land, his home, his habits, in the hope that as an expatriate he may have greater opportunities to rethink, reevaluate, and redefine his place and role under the sun."[30]

Is this true of our students? Do they feel compelled to become strangers to their own home cultures, to "find themselves" apart from their pasts? Do they want to fabricate a new, more cosmopolitan, seemingly sophisticated way of life? If so, might they overreach, becoming disconnected from their roots—even from any roots?

Perhaps, for the purpose of becoming educated in a new place, our students end up disconnected from meaningful locales. Wiesel says that the lost stranger "is always on the run. Everywhere he leaves one more mask, one more memory. In order to become a total stranger, he must reject the last vestiges of his former self."[31] Do our students sometimes become lost runners, seeking careers somewhere, anywhere, disconnected from their own faith traditions, churches, and people? Can we address this potential problem in a digital world, where it's far easier to text a message afar than to set foot in a "strange" nearby community?

Moreover, some college communities are estranged from nearby neighborhoods. Inviting local residents to our classes to share their experiences and wisdom is a wonderful gift for them and our students. So is student volunteering at local churches and other nonprofit organizations as well as working in the community. We servant teachers need a vision for how our work integrates students into communities beyond campus. Without it, we too can become strangers to the locales to which God has called us.

Reflection

How might you give students a vision for local community engagement for their lives ahead?

16

Teach from Your Strengths

During my decades in Christian higher education, I rarely conversed with colleagues about personal teaching gifts or talents. While mentoring faculty at various schools, however, I learned that focusing on faculty giftedness is critically important for servant teachers.

I suggest that we shape our pedagogy partly according to our individual giftedness. We need to identify what we personally can and can't do well, and then pursue teaching practices that are most fitting for us. In my view, this is partly how servant teaching unfolds as calling.

After all, God arranges gifts to contribute to the diversity of church community so that each of us can serve the other members well (e.g., Rom. 12:6–8). I believe that God similarly gives pedagogical gifts for the sake of faith-based educational communities. No single educational approach equally serves all students, courses, or academic majors. Supervising a lab session is very different from teaching an internship course, managing an independent study, and co-teaching a large, lecture-based freshman course. Teaching online and teaching residentially require somewhat different gifts. In other words, academic communities flourish with a variety of gifts for many different educational situations.

One way to address this need is to try different educational practices to see which ones we can do well to the benefit of our students and our institutions. In other words, experience and related self-reflection are critically important. We need to be courageous enough to try new and even challenging practices, knowing that sometimes we will fail. And we must be honest with ourselves, considering feedback from students and colleagues, to gain a clear, realistic sense of our abilities. Then we can excel at those things we can learn to do well and avoid inflicting needless hardship on our students and ourselves.

I am a fine lecturer. I believe I am an excellent grader of essays; I can critique students' prose compassionately yet carefully and helpfully. I think I am good at preparing students for final exams, although it took me years to refine the practice. And I believe, along with Wendell Berry, that to use gifts "less than well is to dishonor them and their Giver."[32] So I continue developing my best abilities, learning from mistakes and celebrating victories.

I am inept at writing multiple-choice exams. I know the theory behind doing it well, but could never master it. I needed colleagues to review my multiple-choice exams to help me avoid the pitfalls that frustrated students and me. I would get defensive even when students would rightly challenge my exam questions. I eventually decided to give only a few multiple-choice exams even though they are less time consuming to grade. If the course material fits a multiple-choice format really well, I will struggle through the process, painstakingly writing and reviewing each question. I hired a gifted test writer to compose multiple choice questions for use with my public speaking textbook.

I know that using student groups outside of class is one of my biggest weaknesses. I simply can't seem to provide the right amount of direction and organization along with patient nurturing of such groups. As a result, students are not well served and I worry about their work; it's a lose-lose situation. But I can work well with student groups during class, so that's what I do.

What if we can't excel at something that seems to be essential for our teaching? We can't teach solely from one or two strengths. Perhaps lecturing is the best example. Not everyone can become a first-rate public speaker, especially for fifty-minute intervals. We can, however, learn to use a combination of practices—such as board outlines, discussion/responses, handouts, and slides along with reasonable clarity, enthusiasm, and expressiveness—to do the job effectively. Moreover, we can parlay our strengths at other practices, such as employing short videos by excellent presenters, to compensate for our less-than-superior lectures. Breaking down material into smaller chunks usually works well for many—along with time for questions and discussion. Simply put, we can mix and match our practices in ways that best serve students, combining various pedagogical practices.

After heartfully accepting the call to servant teaching, we will become more sensitive to our teaching strengths and weaknesses, the practices to embrace, combine, and avoid. Then we will begin a journey of refining our self-understandings and practices, with God comforting us, holding us up, and blessing us along the way. We teach not as solo practitioners, but as members of educational communities with a range of gifted colleagues. Students are best served when we all identify and pursue a mix of strengths.

Reflection

Which teaching practices might you excel at, and which ones should you avoid—and why?

17

Laugh with Learners

My department chair called me to his office to discuss a student evaluation of my teaching. "Look at this," he said. The student wrote, "This guy couldn't bench press forty pounds." My chair asked, "What do you think?" I said, "Well, the student is generous. I probably couldn't do thirty-five pounds." He agreed and sent me on my way.

As servant teachers, we can learn to enjoy laughing at ourselves. Humor and humility are two aspects of the same virtue—to be humble enough to laugh with others at ourselves. Such humility might be the second most important servant-teaching virtue, after gratitude. Healthy humor is humility on display for mutual delight. I love the bench press comment. I don't think the student's remark was meant to be nasty; I see it as appreciation for me as an imperfect human being. It reflects a learner who is willing to poke fun at me just as I jested during the course about the foibles of all human communicators, including myself and some of my former students (never by name).

We college instructors tend to think too highly of ourselves at times. After all, we hold considerable specialized knowledge and even snippets of wisdom. Students know far less, we assume; they sit before us in order to learn from us.

Yet all teachers are human beings, created in the image and likeness of God but wildly imperfect, given to assumptions, presumptions, and biases. We professors hold academic airs, frequently on display for our students and the world to witness. As Rabbi Abraham Heschel puts it, our actual knowledge is atomized and fragmented; we sometimes mistake the part for the whole, which only God fully understands.[33] We too easily profess beyond our actual knowledge and wisdom. We like to impress others, especially students.

When I lecture at campuses where students use my public speaking text, they often are assigned to evaluate my speaking. They look for things that might conflict with what I prescribe in my book. It's wonderfully humbling: "Speaker, heal thyself."

Everything that we teach is a small part of the complexity of our disciplines. Sometimes we even disagree with ourselves over time; I wish I could take back some of my early lectures and writings: "Lord, I pray that my former students will forget what I taught that day." In my field of communication, I expect that students will identify my rhetorical foibles. If they feel comfortable sharing their lovingly critical observations with me, I am delighted. We can chuckle together. My verbal weaknesses extend far beyond my weight-lifting abilities.

When I lecture publicly at schools or other venues, some of my former students show up. After the lectures they like to share memories of our time together. What do they most remember? They recall the humor in good-natured teaching, learning, and ribbing. Most of all, they recall the personal stories I told when I made fun of myself in order to convey an important point about the material.

So one of the things I share with new servant teachers is this: Get ready to enjoy a lifetime of laughs. Accept that you'll both educate and entertain, make profound points and make a fool of yourself—often one right after the other. Enjoy it. Fear less, laugh more.

When I conduct precourse questionnaires (see the appendix), I ask students who their favorite professor was, and why. Their answers usually focus on likability; students connect with teachers who demonstrate that they enjoy students. Such likability is humility in action. Two-way likability is all about teachers and students being human. Instructors and learners thereby witness the profound gift of human beings appreciating each other as imperfect creatures who delight in each other. We have to be sensitive so we don't offend or belittle one another, but we also have to be able to joke around appropriately.

One of the difficult-to-express truths about servant teaching is that it requires a self-reflective openness to the joy of being human learners together with students. I began my teaching career being too serious about everything, rarely cracking a smile; students felt intimidated, fearful, and worried. Trying to excel without adequate humor, I was filled with my own ideas, concepts, opinions, and convictions. As Henri Nouwen puts it, I was infected by a "poverty of mind," without heart.[34] I had little inner space for the shared humanness that transcends my own serious plans and actions. I was a skinny guy loaded with myself. As I shucked my airs—or tried to—my students warmed up to my humbler self. We began laughing together.

Reflection

How might humor—and humility—help you connect with students as a servant teacher in your discipline and courses?

18

Teach Learning

I attended a respected high school but never really learned to study. I skated through courses by doing the minimum necessary for a passing grade. After all, I was busy dealing with family issues and I didn't know how to approach academics.

My second semester in college was a turning point. I had a C− average. I could have sought academic help on campus, but I was too embarrassed and stubborn.

I can remember halfway through that second semester telling myself that I had to figure out how to study, take exams, write papers, and the like. I spent that term learning through trial and error. For instance, I recall rewriting my notes after each class, making them understandable, determining what I actually knew and didn't know from the scribbles. Before long I was typing notes after class and then asking clarification questions at the next class.

During the second week of classes, I tell my students about my turnaround from class attendee to actual learner, about how I began taking responsibility for my learning. I mention that I will be making suggestions during the term about how best to learn in my course. My tips might help in other courses as well.

For example, I review a paragraph in the syllabus about how to take notes when I lecture: (1) follow the outline that I hand out or write on the board, (2) write down all definitions, (3) highlight anything that I say is "important to know," (4) rewrite notes after class the same day, and (5) prepare questions to ask at the next class, either from the reading or the previous lecture-discussion.

Also, I show students a pocket briefcase (it holds index cards) I carry around to make notes to myself about anything I am reading or observing in life. I want them to see that learning is lifelong, cumulative, and driven largely by two things: curiosity and memory. We need to remain curious, even cultivate it, and exercise our memories to review what we are learning.

During the term I explain that visualization is essential for memory—and why I therefore write and mark up notes on the board, using caps, underlines, circles, different colors, even things like stick figures and redundant punctuation. Here's a question I ask students that makes the point: "Have you ever been taking an exam and remembered where the answer was on the page of the text—you could 'see' it—but you couldn't remember what the actual words of the answer were?" Every student has this experience. Much of our learning requires us to "see" what we are learning, preferably in our personalized drawings and writings.

When I began typing my course notes in college, I would then review them with markups, especially different colors, circles, and underlines. In other words, I personalized my notes and began remembering everything on the pages. Not all students are as visually oriented as I am; still,

I personally want to inspire and motivate learners to determine what works best for them.

When a student is struggling with my quizzes or tests, I ask them to bring their notes and the text to meet with me. Almost invariably, the notes are disorganized, incomplete, and unmarked. Moreover, the textbook includes at most yellow highlighting, which normally is insufficient for memory.

To help students even more, I give them copies of not only past tests, exams, and quizzes, but sample papers and projects completed by actual students (with permission and names removed). I review in class the samples as we cover some of the same material, connecting how I am lecturing and discussing with how I evaluate students. Lights start going on in students' minds as they begin learning what I had to discover by trial and error.

When it comes to teaching students how to read the text, I use this simple question for them to ask themselves as they read: "What is the question the text is trying to answer?" I suggest that each section of a text is attempting to answer a question; we won't remember the answer unless we can connect it to the implied question. Otherwise, students tend to think of the text merely as bits of information.

In the "mystagogical" tradition of Christian worship, the leader explains the "mystery" behind what the congregation is doing while doing it. Jesus did so at the Last Supper, explaining it while performing it (Matt. 26:17–30). In a sense, much of our servant teaching should be "mysta-pedagogical," teaching the mystery of learning partly by explaining it as it's happening.[35]

Reflection

How might you teach learning in your courses, perhaps based on your own learning experiences?

19

Affirm Student Giftedness

In a senior writing course I penned the following on a student's paper: "Keep it up—you're a gifted writer!" The student came to see me. "What did you mean"? he asked. I said something like this, "I just meant what I wrote. You can write well. I love to read your work." He responded, "Well, I am graduating this semester and no one ever said that to me before." He became a writer.

How can a student complete college and not discover at least some of their gifts? For one thing, students often select academic majors in order to pursue a field that they think they will like, not one in which they would likely do well. A majority of college graduates end up in a field different than their academic majors. For another thing, students even at Christian universities are not encouraged to develop their abilities as much as to pursue what they want to do, their self-identified calling.

Christian higher education is not set up to help most students discover their gifts. Our schools emphasize student choice in a marketplace of academic programs. Such freedom is wonderful, but it doesn't automatically serve students well.

A freshman came to my office to introduce himself as a new advisee. I was impressed with his courage. He asked me how he could become the next Steven Spielberg (one of the most successful Hollywood film producer-directors of all time). I asked, "Why do you want to be like him?" He responded, "Because I want to impact the movies for Christ." By the end of his freshman year, I knew he simply didn't have the relevant gifts for that field. Of course, there are many other ways to impact the world for Christ; his heart was set on one way that seemed to be out of tune with his gifts.

In order to help students better estimate their potential giftedness, I ask them to take career inventories on campus (e.g., the Strong Interest Inventory). This is a good first step for many to gain a realistic view of themselves.

I also employ an essay assignment that revolutionized my senior seminar. I ask students to conduct three informational interviews with professionals in their field of interest—with a twist. Students have to determine from the interviewees what is required to do well in the profession, and then to compare and contrast those requirements with their own apparent abilities. Specifically, students write an essay about the skills, knowledge, and traits required—compared to theirs. Finally, students explain to me (and themselves) what they can do to close the gap between the required skills, knowledge, and traits and their own current status in all three.

Results are sobering. Many students realize for the first time that they might not fit with their perceived calling. Some discover that there is a Spielberg syndrome in their dreams, apart from created reality. Unfortunately, I employed this assignment only with seniors. By then it was too late for most of them to change academic direction. And I never discovered a way to conduct the same round of informational interview assignments earlier in my college's curriculum. I hope others will pick up that task by building gift-discovering student activities or assignments earlier in the college experience.

Perhaps we can best serve our students by watching for signs of their giftedness across the core and discipline-specific curricula—and affirm our students as appropriate. Most learning involves skills, knowledge, and traits—the three most important general categories for self-assessment. Moreover, students' root abilities in these three areas are widely transferable across career fields.[36]

For instance, a student came to see me about becoming a film writer. He could compose narratives reasonably well, but not with passion and depth. I noticed that he was tremendously organized in his life, not just in his schoolwork. I asked him about producing films instead of writing them. He had no idea what producers do, but soon researched it and interviewed some producers, discovering a required combination of organizational and interpersonal gifts. He became a successful film producer. I simply affirmed his transferable abilities along the way.

Augustine wrote to Volusianus, a pagan: "Your mind and power of expression are so exceptional that you must use them to benefit others too."[37] Shall we affirm our Christian students equally well?

Reflection

How might you help your students identify their own true giftedness?

20

Nurture Student Growth

W e and our students share a problem—namely, the tyranny of the urgent. For most students, especially those who are less organized, college is like the whack-a-mole game at carnivals. Students are focused just on whacking the next-due assignment popping up on their schedules. By the time they receive the graded assignment back, they are already trying to clobber the next mole.

I would like to address the topic of student academic growth. How do we know that students are learning progressively from assignment to assignment? As they play whack-a-mole, they tend to focus on individual, next-due assignments and imminent tests without looking back on and learning from their previous work. For instance, students might not be growing as writers and speakers within and across courses, term to term, and throughout their college careers.

Accrediting agencies and many university administrators support academic assessment because it seems to offer a way of documenting what students are learning over time.

But top-down assessment, as a one-size-fits-all approach, can be very time consuming, subjective, and frustrating.

I believe that the best assessment is organic, occurring naturally as we servant teachers facilitate student growth. Moreover, I think we can do it in ways that reduce our busy-work and enhance student learning.

Consider a spiritual growth metaphor: Churches look for ways of nurturing growth, formally and informally. We know that youth, in particular, are not likely to grow in the faith simply by regurgitating doctrinal information or memorizing Scripture even if they do it well. Such practices can help, but to young people such tasks often seem like playing whack-a-mole.

The same problem exists in much of our teaching and grading. Many students seem to be memorizing things temporarily for grades, not internalizing them for progressive growth. They see each assignment as an isolated task that has to be done in and of itself; some students' goal is freedom from the requirement.

So I developed a way of nurturing student growth within my classes, documenting what students are learning from papers and projects. This solved some of my assessment needs at the same time (assessment related specifically to exams is a different issue).

The procedure is straightforward: I create at least three consecutive and parallel assignments using the same basic grading rubrics.

For instance, students in my media criticism class write three short examples of faith-based media criticism. The writing and content rubrics are the same for all three essays. They get to pick the particular media artifacts to critique; they also select an audience, often a medium like the campus paper or literary magazine, a periodical or website they read online, or even a particular church or Christian school newsletter.

My grading rubrics include writing—a solid thesis, organization, punctuation, and the like. My rubrics also include content-related criteria, such as having to address three basic aspects of media criticism in order: explanation, interpretation, and evaluation.

Here's the key: The student has to submit with each subsequent paper a simple form in which they explain how they have addressed the strengths and weaknesses of the previous paper(s) as indicated by my grading. They also resubmit the previous graded paper with the new one so I can see that they have indeed addressed the relevant strengths and weaknesses in the follow-up paper.

The students' third and final submissions must include the two previous, graded papers along with their explanations of how they addressed my negative and positive comments on those earlier papers—and, of course, an explanation of how they addressed all previous comments in the last paper. I am helping them assess themselves and identify their own progress. This encourages them.

My goal as a servant teacher is to help students become self-reflective assessors of their own work. This helps break the cycle of students focusing only on the next-due assignment without learning progressively from assignment to assignment. My students rarely demonstrate the same level of weaknesses from essay to essay or project to project. They overcome their whack-a-mole addiction. Their papers are progressively better, and I spend less time grading each subsequent one. My comments become increasingly positive, encouraging, and even enthusiastic. Moreover, I can share copies of the papers with assessment administrators as samples of proven student growth.

Reflection

How might you use parallel assignments to organically assess your students' progress and ease your grading?

21

Evaluate Yourself

Faculty who score well on end-of-term student course evaluations believe that such instruments are valid and helpful. Those teachers who score poorly generally do not. Moreover, many of my students dislike filling out such evaluations; they don't provide a lot of specific, written feedback.

I struggled to assess the benefits of such evaluations. By the time I received the results I was usually well into planning and sometimes even teaching the next term. The gap seemed to work against timely personal growth. Also, the questions seemed too generic to be immediately helpful for me and my specific courses.

So I decided to take a bold step forward into the scary land of student evaluation. I would be proactive, not reactive; timely, not delayed. Finally, I would make self-assessment an ongoing process rather than a single, end-of-term practice.

I commend the following practice to you. Please try it, adapting it as needed. You might never have to worry about end-of-term evaluations again.

Beginning at the completion of the second week of a term, with about four minutes left in class, I distribute blank index cards and ask students for "quick feedback." I say something like this: "I am grateful for the chance to teach all of you this term, and I know we can do even better if you give me some honest feedback. Please don't write your names on the cards. Just jot down short responses to these four questions (which I write on the board as well): First, what is going well in the course? Second, what is not going so well? Third, what can I (the teacher) do better? Fourth, what can you (the student) do better?"

The first time you do this you'll be amazed. Suddenly you'll be listening to students in a new, servant-oriented way. You'll hear from students' hearts how they are experiencing your teaching and the course overall. And you'll realize that you have time to address their responses before end-of-term regrets. At the same time, you'll discover what God is already accomplishing through you.

I place a chair near the classroom door for the students to put their completed cards on, blank side up. I immediately go to the hallway (to maintain student privacy in the classroom as they complete their cards). I collect the cards once the last student has left the classroom.

I review the cards that day. One by one, slowly. I ask God to be with me since I might discover comments that bruise my ego. There are also some wonderful, affirming comments. God is good! Then I look for themes across the cards. What am I doing that my students appreciate? I need to do even more of that. What am I doing that is causing student frustration? A typical comment when I started doing this was, "Can you make it clear what we are supposed to know?" Another: "Why do you let the same students talk all the time?" Yet another: "I don't like the readings. Boring. How do they relate to your lectures, anyway?" This is a classic: "Dump the pop quizzes."

Students say revealing things about what they can do better: "Keep up with readings." "More sleep." "Take better notes."

I report my findings at the next class. I summarize the cards and read a few comments—positive and negative. Then I explain how I will be addressing the comments—what I can do better. For instance, the student responses led me to write pop quizzes that include questions which will be on the next exam (see chapter 11). I might suggest that students who indicated a particular problem should see me: "If you indicated that taking notes on my lectures is difficult, please contact me so I can help."

Sometimes the cards reveal that students as a whole disagree about what I am doing well and poorly—usually the latter. In this case, at the next class, instead of giving a report I ask for three volunteers (or I appoint them) to review the cards and give a report at the next class with their own, group suggestions. This is a terrific learning exercise for the class overall as well as for the particular student reviewers. And it creates a stronger sense of students' responsibility for their own learning. Of course, I have the final word. But students have spoken and we all have listened.

Normally, I repeat this process about four times each term. By the last one, hardly any instructor-related problems are identified. Most importantly, I really don't need the end-of-course student evaluations to try to figure out retro-spectively how students reacted specifically to me and my course. I already know far more than those evaluations could tell me. I gently remind students to work on their own weaknesses as well.

Reflection

How might you listen regularly to students in order to become a better servant teacher—and what do you think you would hear?

22

Grade Fairly

I was reviewing in class the results for a multiple-choice exam. I wrote the grading curve on the board. A student raised his hand and said, "Dr. Schultze, your curve is so tight that only a few points make the difference between a B− and an A−. It just seems unfair, especially since our financial aid depends on our grades."

The curve was tight. I struggle to write multiple choice exams. I try to make up for my deficit by throwing out any questions that over half the students get wrong—a practice I adopted for all of my exams regardless of the format. I also gave extra credit for those who got tossed-out questions correct, after establishing the grading curve.

I have always challenged my own grading in terms of fairness, regardless of the assignment or exam. I recall times as a student when I felt unfairly graded because I had spent considerable time on a project only to receive a grade that seemed to belie my effort. I remain sensitive to student complaints, such as, "This grade seems unfair. I worked so hard." At times, students work diligently but simply miss the mark on the purpose and rubrics for assignments. Then I let students redo an assignment with no penalty. If a student works diligently but does poorly on an exam, I review the work personally with the student to see how he or she was interpreting my questions and to determine how the student studied for it. Often I can make helpful suggestions about studying for the next one, including joining a study group.

When it comes to the entire college grading enterprise, I ponder Micah 6:8—doing justice, loving mercy, and walking humbly with God. Practicing it is confounding. I try.

First, I urge students to meet with me if they feel unfairly graded. I hope to forestall resentments, determine how to help the student on subsequent work, and hold myself accountable for my own weaknesses.

Second, I want to help students do their best. In fact, I aim for all students to receive excellent grades. Aiming high helps me focus on serving students.

Third, I offer flexibility in assignments in order to match my requirements to student interests, motivation, and giftedness. For instance, if a junior is a struggling writer but a fine video or in-person presenter, I might let them meet the paper requirement with a video or presentation. I announce this a few times when discussing forthcoming required assignments in class: "If you think this assignment might be a major burden for you, please set up a time to talk with me about it." I discover that the student concern often has to do with learning disabilities, anxiety about particular kinds of assignments, or fear of failure based on past experiences. Sometimes cross-cultural issues are relevant. When I give an essay exam, I often provide extra time for nonnative English speaker/writers and anyone else who requests it in advance.

If a student tells me they are a poor writer, I might offer to personally guide them through the writing process to help them gain skill and confidence. This is especially common for freshmen and international students.

Is such flexibility fair—even just? Am I bending to student weaknesses, perhaps even when the best way to serve students is to require them to do something that they can't yet do well? From my view, this is indeed a potential problem with no simple solution. Each case is different. Mercy often transcends formal rules.

Fourth, I sometimes ask particularly gifted students to work harder—to develop their evident gifts even more. I do it gently, with plenty of encouragement: "I would love to see you further explore this assignment. I know that you can develop your abilities even more. What do you think?"

Fifth, I give students an opportunity to challenge my grading. They just have to submit to me at the next class a written rationale, such as how they interpreted my question.

Servant teaching is a subjective practice, including grading. We have to make tough decisions about how best to serve struggling and outstanding students alike. How can we motivate and encourage them? These are decisions we have to make in each situation after hearing a learner's case, including their academic history, anxieties, and gifts.

Grading raises so many issues for servant teachers that I have to admit my wisdom is limited and my advice is both idiosyncratic and tentative. Maybe the best we can do is to follow Micah's lead together, in community, with faculty and students in ongoing dialogue.

When the student challenged my grading curve on the exam, I made one more change: I told students that when I calculated final grades, I would increase the course grade of any student who was within two points of the grading curve cutoff. I have continued this practice for years.

Reflection

How might you grade fairly—perhaps in the light of Micah's challenge for us to humbly apply justice with love?

23

Offer Service Credit

A student asked me about earning extra credit for showing in class a couple of short YouTube videos related
to the course. When I reviewed the videos, I was struck
by how well they captured course themes. Moreover, the
student enjoyed serving the class and receiving peer recog-
nition as well as academic credit.

The student also served future students since I continued
using some of the videos in online and residential classes.
The episode convinced me that I should encourage students
to serve classmates and me with "service credit," a form of
extra credit.

The general idea of extra credit can be confusing and
challenging. Some faculty use it to help students who hav-
en't been able to keep up with course readings, assignments,
and perhaps attendance. Others use it to encourage excellent
students to do more. I do both.

Giving extra credit seems unfair, however, unless we
offer it to all students, in which case we will be doing even
more additional work, including determining what merits

extra credit, managing the process (e.g., how much extra credit to give and what grading rubrics to use), and of course grading. In other words, extra credit requires additional faculty work. As a servant teacher, I offer students such opportunities regardless of the additional effort required of me.

I have found, however, that one of the best approaches to extra credit is providing opportunities for service credit.

For instance, if I learn that a student (and presumably the entire class) is not being adequately served by the course, I consider how the student (or a group of students) can serve the class without completing a full independent study. For example, a student could produce a video or do a class presentation on careers or another subject related to the course subject; to receive service credit, the student must report findings to the class. My students have addressed how to communicate with persons experiencing depression or anxiety, aphasia, sight limitations, autism, and beyond. They have done excellent presentations on communicating in other cultures, typically using their own experiences. I incorporate some of their material in future courses.

Similarly, students and I developed an effective way of generating engaging class discussions. They find people online who are producing thought-provoking videos about course-related content. Then I invite the video producers to discuss their work via live video with the class. A small group of students handles scheduling and preparing interviews—all for service credit.

Also, as mentioned above, I sometimes use short (3–5 minute) videos in class that students have found online and recommended to me. I vet them and give service credit for those that I use. I also let students work in small groups to find such videos and explain briefly to the class how each video exemplifies or challenges course concepts. I have used such videos in my church, community and academic presentations as well. As students look for these videos, they practice a kind of class-based discernment that enhances their overall learning and serves peers, future students, and me.

I also offer students credit for assisting me with my teaching, public speaking, and writing. For instance, I look for a technologically sophisticated student or two to help me with in-class or online presentations, testing equipment in advance and preparing each session. Some students offer to video or audio record some or all classes and, as needed, record other students' presentations that will be played in class or online. Such students become our technical experts; I expect them to use the technology well and to model a servant attitude. Students have reviewed my book manuscripts and are included in the acknowledgments—even entire classes. I send them signed book copies.

Sometimes a student will ask a great question in class that is beyond my expertise. I might reply, "Wow, that's a wonderful question. I don't know. Would you be willing to earn some service credit by researching it and reporting back soon to the class? If so, please email me or stay for a minute after class so we can discuss it." I review the idea with them and ask them to send me a brief report before the next class to see if the material merits class presentation.

I aim to help students see that learning and teaching are lifelong practices that give meaning to a life of service. Much of Christian higher education is based on students doing their own work just for themselves—for their individual grades and degrees. While that is important, service-related credit can motivate some students to find encouragement and delight in learning. Finally, service credit can build class community.

Reflection

What types of manageable service credit might help you better serve your students, their peers, and you as a community?

24

Promote Hospitality

Some years back, I switched from conducting regular office hours to announcing irregular "café hours." I alert students several mornings a week, usually by text message, where and when I will be "hanging out" that day in a cafeteria or café. I bring along work in case no one shows up.

My student contact increases, enabling me to address student questions and problems long before most students have the courage to come to my office. By adapting to students' ways of communicating and meeting, I have far fewer end-of-the-semester issues. Student grades increase, especially on papers and projects, and my semester-long grading time and discomfort decrease.

Moreover, I nurture stronger student relationships. International students, especially Asians, are far more likely to meet with me during café hours than office hours; the conversations also help us overcome linguistic and cultural hurdles. I see that students work harder for teachers who demonstrate that they care about students. It increases my student retention.

Hospitality, an ancient Judeo-Christian practice, is intimately related to teaching and learning, including pedagogy.[38] David I. Smith writes, "A pedagogy is a home in which teachers and students can live together for a while, a place to which students are welcomed as guests and in which they can grow."[39] Hospitality is about "making room" in our minds, hearts, and spaces for others, especially those who are individually, generationally, and culturally different from us.[40] Such hospitality is essentially the love of Christ incarnate in how we see and treat "strangers" (Heb. 13:1–2).

In education, hospitality includes how we imagine and treat those who are not entirely like us. It's about "listening" to our textbook authors, special guests, the creators of films and novels that we incorporate in our classes, and so much more. In short, have we opened our hearts and minds so that we don't automatically reject the people and ideas we need to understand in order to be God's ambassadors in the world (2 Cor. 5:20)?

As I see them, hospitality and diversity are related. We can't practice hospitality without listening to different persons and cultures. We can't grow in wise discernment if we put our heads in the sands of our own Christian churches and schools. I discovered that I need to be particularly sensitive toward the Christian traditions represented by my students. Some Roman Catholic students confided in me that they were uncomfortable with how I framed theological arguments about Christians' use of icons in the history of the church. They helped me learn more about Catholic views and taught me greater sensitivity.

I know that using words like "evangelical" and "Pentecostal" can cause confusion during my lecture-discussions. Stereotypes don't help us build hospitable learning communities. I have to define things carefully and be sensitive to how different audiences will interpret my words, vocal inflections, and gestures.

As I meet privately with students at Christian universities during my academic program reviews, I find that a growing number of them feel that their teachers are not hospitable to students' varied cultural backgrounds. The issue involves culture more than theology. Students get a sense that instructors look down on learners' "simplistic" understandings of the world. Students often sense, rightly or wrongly, faculty arrogance. They sometimes feel that academic culture, as represented by some highly degreed teachers who lecture but rarely discuss, disrespects their own cultural backgrounds.

Eating together promotes hospitality. I invite students to my home for a meal, sometimes in smaller groups. I bring food to class, varying the types and sources, such as apples and oranges from different regions. I share a thought about the role of each food in other cultures. And I invite students to bring to class foods that have meaning for their families and cultures, always cautioning them to avoid common food allergies.

Like the desert fathers, we should receive our students in hospitality and let them go in peace.[41] This requires mutual respect, reciprocity without obligation, love without legalism, and listening with discernment rather than immediate judgment. This kind of open, peace-giving hospitality nourishes servant-teaching pedagogy, even through campus-café hours.

Reflection
How might you practice hospitality as a servant teacher?

25

Cultivate Civil Discourse

On the second day of class, I get students involved in group activities so they begin to get to know each other.

I distribute nametags for students to fill in and wear. I circle around the room, listening in and matching faces with names. Sometimes I divide students into pairs and ask them to learn enough about each other to introduce one another to the class, including one unusual fact.

This makes it easier for us to begin building relationships. We feel less awkward when we know something about one another and can freely use our names. I am always uncomfortable when in class one student refers to another one with a pronoun. I generally restate the student's comment or question, using the classmate's name. "So, Tony, what do you think about Pat's comment that lying to protect confidentiality can be ethical?"

Cultivating a climate for civil discourse is essential in Christian higher education. I believe that we are called to help students discern controversial events, language, and topics. How else can I address communication-related topics such as obscenity, profanity, news bias, verbal abuse, and gender pronouns? I don't think we are fair to our students and their parents if we allow fear to interfere with pursuing the worthy goal of understanding the world's fallenness.

Still, we have to do it with considerable discernment and humility. How we discuss controversial issues, then, is critically important. The best discussion practices can reduce students' and our fears and promote open, civil dialogue. I have discovered that I have to be intentional about creating a conducive atmosphere for such discussions.

First, before addressing controversial topics, I focus the first two weeks of the term on building classroom community. We as a community first must respect, trust, and simply enjoy one another. Noncontroversial discussions help. This is especially important for online discussions.

Second, I eventually approach controversial topics by defining contrasting perspectives—not taking a stand. As a classroom community, we need to agree on the different views and assumptions held by groups before we can reasonably discuss the topic.

Third, I sometimes give students blank index cards to articulate their views anonymously before beginning discussion. I collect the cards and read each one without favoring any perspectives. The comments give us a sense of what we will face as discussants.

For instance, I asked students to write on cards what the phrase "people of color" means to them (part of the study of semantics). Some students assumed it meant every non-Caucasian person. Others assumed it referred to African Americans. Just by using the cards to review different meanings, we made progress. Discussion was open and lively but not contentious.

Fourth, I tend to stay away from extremely controversial topics that are buzzing in the news headlines. The battle lines are already drawn. Emotions are raw. I used to feel obligated to serve students by addressing the most immediately controversial issues related to my field of communication. More often than not, those discussions did not go well. There is a time for everything (Eccl. 3:1).

Fifth, I admit my biases: "This is how I've been thinking about the topic as a Christian. What are your thoughts? Maybe we can deepen our understandings together. Remember that I will not grade you based on whether or not you agree with my view. I could be wrong."

Sixth, I assume that students differ emotionally. Not all will react the same way to emotional topics. For instance, sometimes I give students an option to view one of two films that convey the same theme but with different levels of potentially offensive content. My goal is to avoid creating emotional distress or causing students to stumble in faith.

Finally, I share with students some of my own vulnerability and self-censorship. I was listening to a group of male students discussing a popular new war film before class; they were highlighting gory details. One of them asked if I had seen it yet. "No," I said. "And I probably won't. I can't handle a lot of violence, perhaps because of my upbringing." I hoped that my comment would serve as an invitation to freedom from group pressure.

We servant teachers face considerable challenges in an uncivil climate in both church and society. We understandably fear upsetting students and parents. So we have to establish civil means of promoting some difficult conversations with and among our students. In my experience, cultivating civil discourse starts on day one as we begin forming community.

Reflection

How might you encourage civility as you promote discourse even on controversial issues for which we and our students need discernment?

26

Tell Stories

"All the world's a stage," says the character Jacques in Shakespeare's *As You Like It*. So is every classroom or online platform. We servant teachers are the lead performers, telling stories about our disciplines.

Of course, lecturing has pedagogical limitations. Hours-long evening or weekend classes are demanding; no one can present that long and hold student attention, let alone promote deep learning. A typical student's attention span has declined over my teaching career; I now assume it's about ten minutes.

So we necessarily vary our pedagogical practices, from lectures to class discussions, and from group discussions to student presentations. We try guest presenters and video presentations. Yet we still have to "instruct" in a lecture mode. Even if we record ourselves for a flipped classroom, where students view the lecture outside of class and discuss it during class sessions, we have to figure out which presentational practices will work well.

I have probably worked on my lecturing (presenting, generally speaking) more than any other pedagogical practice, knowing that it's crucially important not just for my classroom and online workshops/webinars, but also for my live and recorded video presentations, church speeches, academic lectures, and civic engagements.

The most important thing I have learned is that stories are essential for our presentational pedagogy. Narrative is the most powerful form of instructional communication; it can engage and teach simultaneously, like parables. When I start losing students' attention, I know I've failed to present material in the form of a story for too long. I am just shoveling information without an engaging narrative context.

As servant teachers, we can present material effectively through four types of narratives: (1) the story of the original discovery of the material we are teaching, (2) the story of our own discovery or use of the material discovered originally by others, (3) the story of how others have applied the material, and (4) God's overarching narrative—biblical history—as it informs and contextualizes the material.

First, every main concept we teach has a storied history. Who discovered or defined it? When? Where? Why? How did rat poison become a human blood thinner? How did humans discover the earth was not the center of the universe? How and why did a method of accounting or engineering emerge? From my field: Who first defined communication as transmitting rather than sharing—and why?[42]

Second, we teachers somehow learned others' concepts—maybe as the concepts were taught to us or we read about them. How did our revelation of others' discoveries inform and perhaps even change us? I found the deepest meaning of listening (as "attending to reality") by reading about the biblical distinction between a wise person who understands reality before speaking, and a foolish person who speaks before listening (the Hebrew distinction is reflected in James 1:19). I can engage students profitably for forty minutes just on the significance of that biblical distinction, using mini-stories along the way as examples and illustrations.

Third, we can tell stories about family, friends, colleagues, pastors, and beyond who learned something about our subject through their life experiences. My psychiatrist said, "When you have adult children you become a consultant; never offer advice unless asked for it." The academic literature supports his point, which I teach partly through stories of my own miscommunication with adult offspring. I learned how to listen well to my grown children thanks to warning kicks from my wife under the kitchen table.

Fourth, Scripture contextualizes all truth for those who have ears to hear it—who are wise enough to listen. Prooftexting is dangerous; we might miss the real biblical context and meaning. But the narratives of the Bible—including the overarching story of creation, fall, redemption, and renewal—can help us engagingly contextualize much of what we teach, from the humanities to social and natural sciences, and from art to engineering. All of our disciplines come alive in the context of biblical wisdom. In this sense, there is nothing new under the sun even for learned academicians (Eccl. 1:9).

We teachers, created in God's image and likeness, perform our work on God's stage. We even use the narrative-based pedagogical practices that Jesus employed to engage audiences. We teach with stories by our nature as well as by pedagogical necessity.

Reflection

How might stories help you to engage students in your discipline?

27

Use Media Fittingly

I prefer teaching in classrooms where projection screens are situated in a front corner—not at the front center, where the whiteboard is usually located. This allows me to walk toward the other side of the front, diverting student attention away from the screen and toward me or the whiteboard. Alternatively, I use a screen mute button to turn off the projector and refocus student attention on me, the board, a paper handout, a discussion, or anything else.

The use of projection screens is a helpful metaphor for how we servant teachers can approach all media practices— fittingly. This involves using the most fitting media for each instructional purpose. We can use a variety of high- and low-tech media—all of the media developed by humans as part of the unfolding of God's original creation.

Media include all of the instructional means and methods at our disposal. We teachers ourselves are media, employing our verbal and nonverbal expressiveness; every-thing we use to communicate with students might be a fitting medium in some situations.

When I enter a classroom or an online class session, I see myself partly as the regulator of fitting media. I need a plan that indicates which ones to use, when, and how. My concern is not whether or not to use media, but how to select and employ them fittingly from available options.

For instance, I usually send students editable handouts in advance of classroom or online use. Some students will print out the documents to write on them. Others will edit the documents on their computers or pads during class. Students can decide which method is a better fit for them; I can empower students to use the best media practices for their own learning.

When I start planning a class session, I review possible media combinations, from index cards to screen pro-jections, whiteboards, and lectures. Sometimes I play music on my phone while I project the lyrics on the screen or hand out a paper document with the lyrics. I love using a Bob Dylan song, "Man Gave Names to All the Animals," to capture the playfulness and creativity of human linguistic action as a reflection of God's own creativity.

Toward the end of my senior seminar class, I seek to capture what faithfulness looks like in retrospect, as an aging adult looking back on one's life. This is a difficult instruc-tional task, communicating across generations. I know that I need to teach affectively, creating emotional empathy. I usu-ally conclude the class using the short video montage of country singer Johnny Cash's life. We see images of his life as he sings a Nine Inch Nails song, "Hurt." He sings reflectively, regretfully, toward the end of his life, of his transgressions as well as his fame:

I wear this crown of thorns
Upon my liar's chair

Full of broken thoughts
I cannot repair

I always turn off the room lights to maximize the video's visual and aural impact. When the song is over, the class is always silent. I wait ten seconds, mute the screen image, turn on the lights, thank the students for coming, and dismiss them. After class I send students an email with links to the video (so they can view it again) and lyrics.

Sometimes I hand out paper copies of a short news story or a page or two from a feature article. I ask students to individually read the article, discuss it in small groups, and report their findings to the class via a group spokesperson. The students read, discuss, and present—three media forms. I might even ask them as groups to come up with a one-sentence response and then write it on the board for the entire class to read and discuss. If the class is working toward a consensus, I write the options on the computer, projected on the screen, and edit the consensus sentence for students as they discuss and refine it as an entire class. I serve as the scribe.

We have many media choices. When we aim for a mix of purpose-fitting media—not a single one—we can serve students most effectively. Through trial and error, we can determine what works best, adjusting our pedagogy along the way for each class, assignment, and technology. High-tech methods, such as screen projections, are most effective when used in combination with more traditional, low-tech means, like discussions. As soon as we focus too much on one medium—whether projections or front-of-class lectures, we reduce overall student learning. God created us as creative, multimedia creatures. Moreover, students as individuals learn differently.

Reflection

How might you use a fitting mix of low-tech and high-tech means of teaching to serve students—and how can you know you are doing it well?

28

Record Yourself

I conducted a pedagogical experiment that opened my mind about recording my class presentations. Students were asking me to audio record my lectures and post them on our course management system; sometimes I speak too quickly for notetaking. My colleagues were telling me not to do it because some students might skip class and just listen to recordings. I also wondered about the potential value of posting parts of my lectures publicly to serve a broader constituency. I felt like I was being pulled in various directions, but the safest route seemed to be the status quo.

Then I had a physically challenged student and one with ADHD in the same class. The campus office that served these students asked me to audio record sessions for them; the office would make the recordings available just to the selected learners. I offered instead to distribute the recordings to the entire class via the course management system. Why not give it a try?

I told the class what I was doing and put it in the syllabus, without mentioning any particular students or student needs. I asked the class not to share the recordings with outsiders in order to protect everyone's privacy, particularly when we had discussions. A few times during the semester I edited out some student discussions before posting recordings—and I told the students I did so to protect their privacy. Three things occurred that surprised me that term, changing my view of recording myself.

First, students still attended class. In fact, attendance was strong throughout the term. Absent students didn't ask me what was covered in class ("Did you cover anything important?"). Instead, they apologized for missing class and thanked me for the recordings.

Second, many students relistened to my lectures. They could easily do so while exercising, jogging, driving, and eating. Students told me they were doing this, but I also tracked the number of audio downloads. I assume it helped learners because the overall academic performance of the class was excellent.

Third, student discussion seemed to be better than was typical—more immediate, engaging, and relevant. Apparently, my recordings were generating out-of-class discussion among students; the discussions were carrying over to the classroom, according to student reports.

Fourth, I became more self-conscious about my presentations. Knowing that I was giving students an opportunity to listen to me a second or third time—and talk together about my presentations—I worried that I might not be living up to their expectations. I listened to my own recordings, making notes about what I was doing well or poorly, serving or not serving listeners.

By listening to myself, I discovered ways of improving my presentational organization. I began being more obvious with my transitions between topics. I realized I was presenting too quickly. I slowed down my pacing while increasing my verbal expressiveness.

Since then, I have tried video recording my lectures, but the technology is generally too clumsy to do it well. I still find that having to be in front of the camera at a reasonable distance for solid facial cues, and also capturing my scribbles on the whiteboard, is just too much to manage unless a student follows me with a camera. Even then, I need a wireless microphone I can wear, freeing me up for gesturing, moving around, and writing on the board; the quality of the audio is important to students. Few students told me they watched the videos; they preferred audio with downloadable outlines in editable files.

When I had to miss class to attend a conference during my semester experiment, I audio recorded a lecture in advance. That, too, benefited both the students and me. I learned more about doing a lecture for the microphone without the benefit of video. Since then, however, I routinely video record lectures in advance on my computer if I know I have to be gone. I use a technology that allows me to show a screen and myself at the same time as well as easily shuttle between the two images.

Especially in the age of online education, flipped classrooms, and mixed courses, we should consider recording and re-recording our presentations, refining our communication, and developing a corpus of materials that we can provide to students and perhaps beyond. My experiment started my journey into consistent recording for students' benefit. As a bonus, I became a better presenter by reviewing my own recordings. My original pedagogical experiment changed my mind.

Reflection

How might you better serve students—and yourself—by audio or video recording your presentations?

29

Anticipate the Spirit

I taught at a school that sends a questionnaire to students five years after graduation, asking which professors most positively influenced them. The provost sent me a note with a quote from a former student that credited me with greatly impacting his life.

I remembered the student. He sat slumped in the back row with the bill of his baseball cap pulled over his eyes. I assumed he was napping. I don't think I ever conversed with him outside of class. But his comments to the provost made clear what he had learned in my course, broadly speaking, and how he applied it to his life after graduation. I was astonished.

How shall we understand such a phenomenon pedagogically? Should it make any difference for us to know that God has the last word? I am not suggesting that we ought to be lackadaisical. We can't be servant teachers by opting out of our responsibility for excellence and compassion. But aren't we partnering with Christ, who can do all things through us (Phil. 4:13)?

Eugene H. Peterson says that the Christian faith is not simply about knowing and doing things. It's "a matter of letting God do something for you—letting him love you, letting him save you, letting him bless you, letting him command you."[43] What does that look like in our teaching and in students' learning?

Perhaps we should intentionally provide spiritual space in our teaching. After all, we are not the only factor in students' learning. God is truly at work—the great speech agent of history who spoke the world into existence and speaks to and through his ambassadors. God impacts students' motivation and performance. And he does this partly through us; we are God's speech agents.

We might say something that motivates a particular student. A thought or way of expressing course content might come to us suddenly in class; it might work so well that we make a note to use it in future semesters. I started a practice of making notes to myself on my lecture sheets immediately after each class session so I would not lose the things that I unexpectedly said that seemed to serve students well.

We teach under God as his servants, reaping the benefits of the Spirit's work in and through us. Therefore, we should teach expectantly. We can teach as if with every class meeting and each student appointment the risen Christ will be there ahead of us.[44] Can we imagine this? Anticipate it?

As we acknowledge and act upon God's claim on us as servant teachers, God blesses us and our students. We are called for purposes beyond our immediate understanding. More than we easily recognize, God nurtures communication and community. Gratitude motivates us to remain open to God's work in our teaching and to recall the great things he has already accomplished in our lives. Gratitude and calling together lead us to work under God's direction and mercy even when we see the next class session or semester only darkly.[45] Our Christian spirituality as teachers is about attending to what God has done, is doing, and has promised to do. In this sense, God doesn't want our teaching to be superficially pietistic; he wants a deep, expectant faith to form our teaching and thus students' learning.

In the Western world, we tend to think of time as sequence and duration. The ancient Greeks had two words for time—*chronos* and *kairos* ("kye-ros"). The former was sequential time. The latter meant the right or opportune time. We need a far greater sense of *kairos*.

Kairos is the right time, neither too soon nor too late. Kairos, as I am using it, means the right moment to serve in a particular way—including to speak up or to remain silent, to encourage or challenge. Perhaps the Holy Spirit directs us to seize such moments in and outside the classroom.

The key is for us to be available in the present to see the possibilities for serving others. We are free to say what should be said, when it should be said, to listen when listening is most needed, and to be open to communication beyond our schedules and apparent abilities. Walking with the Holy Spirit is essential for servant teachers. In a sense, the Holy Spirit makes us *kairos* incarnate.

When our hearts are open, anticipating God in our teaching, we begin seeing the work of the Spirit that we once overlooked or even doubted. We realize that we are teaching beyond just our skills. We miraculously teach with the triune God, who journeys with us. Most of the time we witness this retrospectively, as I did with my student in the baseball cap.

Reflection

What practices might help you anticipate, identify, and celebrate the work of the Holy Spirit in your teaching?

30

Conclude Doxologically

On the last day of class, I thank students for the opportunity to be their servant teacher. It's a time of celebration for everything that we have accomplished together.

First, however, I say something surprising: "I would like to apologize to each of you for any ways I have failed you as your professor. I am a fallen creature, and I am sure I let you down. I might have embarrassed you in front of the class. I might have angered you. I might have treated you unjustly because of my imperfect grading. Please forgive me. And know that I completely forgive you for anything you might have said or done that hurt me. Isn't it a wonderful gift to be at a school where we come together in Jesus' name to learn, love, and forgive?"

I conclude each term with the apology followed by a celebration. I ask students to recall together some memorable, especially humorous things that happened during the term. My aim is to contextualize the course in tune with the gospel of Jesus Christ. We all do things that contribute to our students' and our own stress and anxiety. By God's goodness, however, we progress together, teaching and learning. Great things occur. Fun happens. It's time to recall some of the blessings beyond just grades.

I think we servant teachers should end each term with grateful hearts, in tune with chapter 1. We teach by God's provisions. God's everlasting forgiveness toward us plants our imperfect work in the soil of peace. Only God frees us from excessive stress and fear. I hope to end each course doxologically by lightheartedly recalling God's goodness during the term. I suggest a few awards, such as for the person who came to class the latest one day, who brought the most enticing food to eat in class, who could most make us laugh, and so forth. What about me? What was my worst assignment or lecture?

By remembering and celebrating our times together as a class, we find joy and rest. When during the term we smiled and greeted one another with encouraging words, we defied the criticism and cynicism that plague our world, including in higher education. When we rejected our human tendency to self-pity—almost a public artform today—we resisted one of the major temptations of our time, resentment. When we laughed together over my forgetfulness or misspeaking, we enjoyed our humanness. Celebrating God's goodness in everyday education is a powerful antidote to self- and community-nurtured distress.

I anticipate this doxological ending of a course throughout the term. As both a metaphor for faithful living and a pedagogical practice, I plan my class sessions with time to spare. If it's a fifty-minute class, I create a forty-minute lesson plan. If it's a three-hour evening class, I plan for a half hour less. I aim to complete our time together without a last-minute race for the door. This way, my students and I can address any extant confusion and questions, summarize and give thanks for what we have learned, and if appropriate pray for special needs.

I begin this last part of each class session with words such as this: "Thanks so much for your attention and participation today—even in the face of challenges with other courses and your personal life. How can we best serve each other before we depart? Let's make sure we are all on the same grace-filled track before we return to the hustle and bustle around us."

My goal is to remind us that although we sometimes live in a kind of spiritual desert, we are part of God's work toward the new heaven and the new earth (Rev. 21–22). We are not just busy learners; we are agents of renewal who, even while we work, need the kind of rest that comes with forgiveness and celebration. Our lives necessarily include joyful rest, just as God rested on the seventh day of Creation and looked back gratefully at his work (Gen. 2:2).

The word "school" comes from the Latin "schola," which means "free time."[46] The idea was to protect schooling from excessive, outside labor. Ironically, we have turned schools into hectic races toward measured productivity. Perhaps we are even snuffing out the mystery of grace from a God who plants delight around us. Maybe we need to recapture the implications of the gospel of peace for our servant teaching.

Each academic term is a series of beginnings and endings. But the end of a term, above all, is a time for celebrating the goodness that has carried us through yet another round of academic challenges, victories, and delights. It's a time to share stories of our time together with forgiveness, food, and fun. It can be a doxological taste of heaven on earth.

The last thing I say to my students is this: "I have loved teaching you. Each of you is a gift. Thank you."[47]

Reflection

How might you conclude each of your classes and especially the end of a term by offering a taste of heaven on earth?

Appendix: Sample Precourse Questionnaire

(Please fill out the form and save it using your name as the file name. Then send it to me [my email address] as an email attachment *along with a photo of yourself.* Note: I will keep your personal information confidential, but please feel free not to answer any of my personal questions—QS.)

Your full name:
(please include the first name that you would prefer to use in class)

Best email address:
(Please consider using a long-term address, such as gmail, to be used even after graduating.)

Best phone number with area code:

Best text messaging number (If different from above):

Explain which medium you prefer for instructor communication.
1. Email:
2. Text messaging:
3. Other:

Your major/concentration:
Second major/concentration:

Minor:

If you wish you had chosen a different major/concentration, what would it have been? Why?

What has been your favorite class at XXX so far? Why?

Who has been your favorite instructor at XXX so far? Why?

What is the one thing that you most <u>dislike</u> about some courses/instructors that you would like to make sure is *not* evident in this class?

What is the one thing that you most <u>like</u> about some courses/instructors that you would really like to make sure *is* evident in this class?

What would be your ideal career—if you could do anything you wanted? Why?

What do you think might keep you from achieving that goal?

Please describe any experience you have with any of the following (e.g., how much, which technologies, for what purposes): [Note: This is the kind of question I might ask to determine how much experience students already have related to the course subject as well as to identify specific students who might want to help me and the class for service credit, such as helping me with technology (chapter 23).]
1. Blogging (text/writing):
2. Still photography:

3. Website design/posting/uploading:
4. Video production:
5. Audio production:

Are you available to meet before or after class—or both? If not, what are the best days/times to meet with you?

What would you most like the instructor to know about you (e.g., learning style, job, internship, native language, special challenges or gifts, hopes and dreams—all confidential, if you wish to share so that I may serve you more personally)?

Any other hopes or thoughts to share with me as we begin the term together?

About Quentin Schultze

After growing up in Chicago, Quentin Schultze earned a PhD from the Institute of Communications Research at the University of Illinois in Urbana-Champaign. He taught at numerous schools, including thirty-three years at Calvin University, where he served as professor of communication, the Arthur H. DeKruyter Chair in Faith and Communication, and director of the Gainey Institute for Faith and Communication. He received Calvin's Presidential Award for Exemplary Teaching in 2000.

Professor Schultze leads teaching and book-writing workshops for colleges and universities. He has consulted on communication projects for many nonprofit and for-profit organizations. He mentors professionals about their interpersonal (person-to-person) and public communication, including their public speaking. He also conducts communication workshops for employees of small to large organizations. He serves on the board of directors of Baker Publishing Group.

Dr. Schultze's books include *Communicating with Grace and Virtue: Learning to Listen, Speak, Text, and Interact as a Christian*, *An Essential Guide to Public Speaking*, *Résumé 101: A Student and Recent-Grad Guide to Crafting Résumés and Cover Letters That Land Jobs*, *An Essential Guide to Interpersonal Communication*, and *Habits of the High-Tech Heart: Living Virtuously in the Information Age*. His books have won six national awards.

His numerous scholarly publications have appeared in several dozen journals, such as *Business History Review*, *Qualitative Sociology*, and the *Journal of Communication*. He has written over a hundred articles for general-interest periodicals.

Professor Schultze has been quoted in the *The Wall Street Journal*, *Newsweek*, *U.S. News & World Report*, *The Los Angeles Times*, *The New York Times*, *Fortune*, the *Chicago Tribune*, *USA Today*, and many more publications. He has been interviewed by CNN, CBS, NBC, ABC, NPR, and numerous radio and television stations, websites, blogs, and podcasts.

Follow his blog and publications and subscribe to his email list at www.quentinschultze.com.

His YouTube channel is located at https://www.youtube.com/c/QuentinSchultze.

Notes

[1] Nicholas P. Wolterstorff, *Educating for Life: Reflections on Christian Teaching and Learning* (Grand Rapids, MI: Baker Academic, 2002), 158.

[2] My approach to teaching is similar to what Jennifer Lindholm calls a "student-centered teaching method." Jennifer Lindholm, *The Quest for Meaning and Wholeness: Spiritual and Religious Connections in the Lives of College Faculty* (San Francisco: Jossey-Bass, 2014), 210.

[3] James M. Houston, *Joyful Exiles: Life in Christ on the Dangerous Edge of Things* (Downers Grove, IL: InterVarsity, 2006), 106.

[4] Søren Kierkegaard, *Provocations: Spiritual Writings of Kierkegaard*, ed. Charles E. Moore (Farmington, PA: Plough, 1999), 251.

[5] David I. Smith and James K. A. Smith, "Introduction: Practices, Faith, and Pedagogy," in *Teaching and Christian Practices: Reshaping Faith and Learning*, ed. David I. Smith and James K. A. Smith (Grand Rapids, MI: Eerdmans, 2011), 3.

[6] C. S. Lewis, *The Abolition of Man* (San Francisco: HarperSanFrancisco, 2001), 14.

[7] Perry L. Glanzer and Nathan F. Alleman, *The Outrageous Idea of Christian Teaching* (New York: Oxford University Press, 2019), 14.

[8] Henri J. M. Nouwen, *Reaching Out: The Three Movements of the Spiritual Life* (New York: Doubleday, 1975), 49.

[9] Robert K. Greenleaf, *Seeker and Servant: Reflections on Religious Leadership*, ed. Anne T. Fraker and Larry C. Spears (San Francisco: Jossey-Bass, 1996), 64.

[10] Henri J. M. Nouwen, *The Inner Voice of Love: A Journey through Anguish to Freedom* (New York: Doubleday, 1996), 65.

[11] Bernard of Clairvaux, *Selected Works*, ed. and trans. G. R. Evans (New York: Paulist, 1987), 179.

[12] Kierkegaard, *Provocations*, 378. He added, "Christ has desired only one kind of gratitude: the praise that comes from the transformed individual." *Provocations*, 410.

[13] Joseph Sittler, *Running with the Hounds* (Chicago: University of Chicago Campus Ministry, 1977), 63.

[14] I discuss this more fully in Quentin Schultze, *Here I Am: Now What on Earth Should I Be Doing?* (Grand Rapids, MI: Baker Books, 2005), 50–53.

[15] Paul Tournier, *The Adventure of Living*, trans. Edwin Hudson (New York: Harper & Row, 1965), 58.

[16] Quoted in Paul Tournier, *The Person Reborn*, trans. Edwin Hudson (New York: Harper & Row, 1966), 87.

[17] Dietrich Bonhoeffer, *Life Together* (New York: Harper & Row, 1954), 49.

[18] This phrase (in Latin, *fides quaerens intellectum*) is generally associated with Augustine and Anselm.

[19] Henri J. M. Nouwen, *Clowning in Rome: Reflections on Solitude, Celibacy, Prayer, and Contemplation* (New York: Doubleday, 1979), 60.

[20] I borrowed this language from David G. Benner, *Human Being and Becoming: Living the Adventure of Life and Love* (Grand Rapids, MI: Brazos, 2016), 92.

[21] Thomas Merton, trans., *The Wisdom of the Desert: Sayings from the Desert Fathers of the Fourth Century* (New York: Penguin, 1960), 62.

[22] Kierkegaard, *Provocations*, 312.

[23] Nouwen, *Reaching Out*, 18.

[24] Eugene H. Peterson, *Under the Unpredictable Plant: An Exploration in Vocational Holiness* (Grand Rapids, MI: Eerdmans, 1992), 164.

[25] In order to accomplish this, I schedule in advance my personal calendar along with my academic schedule for the entire term, protecting grading time for each assignment.

[26] I also discovered early in my Christian university teaching that a group of students kept files of past exams for many classes, passing them along from year to year. I liked that idea for my courses once I stopped repeating the same exams. I encouraged students to study my past exams and distributed copies of them.

[27] Dietrich Bonhoeffer, *Letters and Papers from Prison*, ed. Eberhard Bethge (New York: Macmillan, 1967), 13. Biologist Kathleen Tallman says that service learning "is the glue that connects knowledge with practice and people." Quoted in Michelle LaPorte, "Academic Service-Learning: Building Connections from Classroom to Community," Azusa Pacific University website, posted November 2, 2018, http:www.apu.edu/articles/academic-service-learning-where-the-cornerstones-connect.

[28] Augustine, *De doctrina christiana* 1.28, 29.

[29] Wendell Berry, *What Are People For? Essays by Wendell Berry* (New York: North Point, 1990), 162–63.

[30] Elie Wiesel, *From the Kingdom of Memory: Reminiscences* (New York: Schocken Books, 1990), 64–65.

[31] Wiesel, *From the Kingdom of Memory*, 65.

[32] Wendell Berry, *Sex, Economy, Freedom & Community* (New York: Pantheon Books, 1992), 113.

[33] Abraham J. Heschel, *Who Is Man?* (Stanford, CA: Stanford University Press, 1965), 114.

[34] Nouwen, *Reaching Out*, 74.

[35] See Brandon Harvey, "The Mystagogical Tradition," *Homiletic and Pastoral Review* website, July 31, 2018, https://www.hprweb.com/2018/07/the-mystagogical-tradition/.

[36] I wrote a résumé-writing book for college students and recent graduates based on the approach of identifying one's skills, knowledge, and traits. Quentin J. Schultze and Bethany Kim, *How to Write Powerful College Student* Résumés *and Cover Letters: Easy Tips, Basic Templates, Sample Formats, and Real Examples That Get Job Interviews like Magic* (Grand Rapids, MI: Edenridge, 2010).

[37] Augustine, *Letters of Saint Augustine: The Words of the Most Celebrated Theologian of the Latin Church*, trans. John Leinenweber (Tarrytown, NY: Triumph Books, 1992), 120. The quoted letter has been catalogued as #137 of Augustine's letters.

[38] See David I. Smith and Barbara Carvill, *The Gift of the Stranger: Faith, Hospitality, and Foreign Language Learning* (Grand Rapids, MI: Eerdmans, 2000).

[39] David I. Smith, *On Christian Teaching*: *Practicing Faith in the Classroom* (Grand Rapids, MI: Eerdmans, 2018), 12.

[40] See especially Christine D. Pohl, *Making Room: Recovering Hospitality as a Christian Tradition* (Grand Rapids, MI: Eerdmans, 1999).

[41] Merton, *Wisdom of the Desert*, 51.

[42] It was probably Protestants, mesmerized by the apparent evangelistic potential of mass media. See James W. Carey, *Communication as Culture: Essays in Media and Society* (Boston: Unwin Hyman, 1989), 14–18.

[43] Eugene H. Peterson, *Traveling Light* (Colorado Springs, CO: Helmers & Howard, 1988), 49.

[44] Pastor Eugene H. Peterson says, "In every visit, every meeting I attend, every appointment I keep, I have been anticipated. The risen

Christ was there ahead of me." Peterson, *Under the Unpredictable Plant*, 127.

[45] The metaphor is based on 1 Cor. 13:12.

[46] See Henri J. M. Nouwen, *Lifesigns: Intimacy, Fecundity, and Ecstasy in Christian Perspective* (New York: Doubleday, 1986), 61.

[47] In my smaller, upper-level courses I sometimes give students a course-related gift. For instance, in my senior seminar, which emphasizes calling, I give them a picture card with a photo of the John Swanson print of *The Conductor*, which I mentioned in this book's introduction. I suggest that my students post the picture where they will see it regularly to remind themselves that they are God's craftsmanship, created in Christ Jesus to do good works that he prepares in advance for them (Eph. 2:10).

Made in the USA
Monee, IL
17 September 2022